Reverend Moon's
Message from Prison

God's
Warning
to the
World

Reverend Moon's
Message from Prison

God's
Warning
to the
World

COPYRIGHT © 1985

ISBN 0-910621-42-X

HSA-UWC
4 West 43rd Street
New York, New York 10036

Distributed by the Rose of Sharon Press

First Printing 1985

Printed in the United States of America

Contents

Introduction

> For Christ did not please himself; but, as it is
> written, 'The reproaches of those who re-
> proached thee fell on me.' For whatever was
> written in former days was written for our
> instruction, that by steadfastness and by the
> encouragement of the scriptures we might have
> hope.
>
> Romans 15:3-4

The trial and imprisonment of Reverend Sun Myung
Moon has been a shock to many people in many different
ways. The United States federal prosecutors were shocked
when he returned from immunity in Korea to deal with the
charges. Unification Church members were shocked at the
treatment accorded Reverend Moon at the trial level, and at
the verdict rendered by the jury. Opponents of religious
freedom were shocked at the unprecedented variety of
churches and lay organizations which supported Reverend
Moon's cause as his case went to the Supreme Court. Those
amici supporters were in turn shocked by the Court's refusal
even to consider the threats the case poses toward religious
freedom in this country.

But the greatest shock of all has been the surge of
cooperation between the Unification Church and other
Christian churches across America since the time of Reverend Moon's imprisonment. Within the community of cler-

gy, interactions with the Unification movement in the arenas of social action, ecumenism, pastoral reflection and religious freedom have brought surprising new stimulation. Ecumenical activities include the National Council for Church and Social Action, the Interdenominational Conferences for Clergy, the Common Suffering Fellowship, and countless local meetings and cooperative ventures. Members of all denominations are praising God for this outpouring of spirit and fellowship. The interracial and interdenominational nature of these activities has generated a refreshing, Christ-centered spirit of love and good will, as well as a sense of new direction for the churches in America.

In this context, many ministers are desirous for some "prison message" from Reverend Moon. Historically many Christian giants, from St. Paul to John Bunyan to Dietrich Bonhoffer and Martin Luther King, have written moving and important works while suffering imprisonment by hostile authorities. As always, Reverend Moon is very prolific in his output of ideas and inspiration while in prison at Danbury. Daily he continues to teach and share his wisdom. In particular he relates to us about the heart of God, and God's concern for this present age. He is thinking also very much about humankind's future; in this vein he is sharing about the need for religious dialogue and harmony for the sake of global peace; about ideal love, and the education of youth for the creation of true, God-centered families; about the spiritual world, and the relationship of the spiritual with the physical realms of life. When with other clergy, Rev. Moon stresses revelation he has received concerning sin and salvation, the life of Christ, and the second coming. As this book is prepared for Christian clergy, we have also emphasized this aspect of Rev. Moon's teachings.

Reverend Moon's mode of production is not the written word—he is a verbal communicator. Even most of the documents pertaining to his teachings were written down by disciples, either from his sermons or direct dictation. His contemporary thoughts, therefore, are recorded in notes gathered by those who can visit him. To make this content available to a larger audience, in particular to the clergy, Reverend Moon consented to some selections from his speeches and sermons being published. The content he is now sharing behind prison walls has a deep continuity with these speeches and sermons. The present volume, then, is a useful compilation of what he is sharing now with visiting ministers and disciples, and constitutes his "message from prison."

Reverend Moon's message is based upon unchanging truth. It is a strong prophetic message directed at America and Christianity. Thus it is a warning from God. Since God is a God of love, the warning is heartfelt, given out of love.

The substructure of this volume consists of three speeches basic to Reverend Moon's message to American Christians, supplemented with excerpts from others of his sermons. Through this process the three speeches "God's Hope for Man," "God's Hope for America," and "The Future of Christianity," were expanded into six messages. The seventh speech here included is his talk to several hundred Unification members at the moment of his departure to Danbury.

A word on how to approach this material. Reverend Moon is speaking as a prophet of God. The prophet's role is to warn, to chastise, to guide, to interpret the Word of God to his contemporary society. The prophet has his primary authority from God, who is speaking through him, and often the message runs counter to social or religious norms safeguarded by religious institutions and theological schools. Reverend Moon is not a trained theologian, motivated by the desire to develop contemporary theological issues. Nor is he motivated by the desire to please this society. He is motivated solely by the desire to proclaim God's truth.

Reverend Moon is an exuberant speaker. He speaks with members for hours on end every day and in every conceivable setting: from formal religious services, to church administrative meetings, to birthday celebrations, to fishing boats or around a campfire. No matter what the setting, his speaking has a great flowing power, ranging over the broadest scope of human and divine reality. Sometimes he will speak for hours and just scratch the surface of his topic, and he will continue with that topic another day. His talks are always characterized by a great deal of give and take with his audience, sometimes sharing delightful humor, other times a profound seriousness and repentance, always a great vision and ideal.

Therefore, proper comprehension of these words, removed from their source as they are by interpretor, translator, one editor, two editors, and probably a lot of atmosphere, requires something special. Reverend Moon refers to that something often throughout the talks printed here. That something is a pure and open heart and a discerning mind, both guided and protected by sincere prayer.

I have been attending Reverend Moon as a disciple for twenty seven years. I am able to visit Reverend Moon in prison at Danbury two or three times a week, listening to him for several hours on each such occasion. I am gratified that this content is now being made available to a wider audience, and yet I am sorry because what you read here is such a small glimpse of Reverend Moon's thought. We look forward to the day when broader areas of his teaching may be published.

I would like to express my thanks to Dr. Tyler Hendricks, who did the editing for this book. May God grant you the inspiration in reading and reflecting upon this book that He has granted us in its preparation.

New York City   Reverend Chung Hwan Kwak
November, 1984

1

God's Ideal For The World

My topic is "God's Ideal for the World." This subject is vast in nature and rather complicated in content. I will try my best to stay on the central point.

Throughout history there have been great philosophies and philosophers who searched for the true meaning of human behavior and happiness. Each one of them must always answer one fundamental question: Does God exist? Every philosophical battle returns ultimately to that one fundamental question and still this question has not been solved. Could a definitive decision be reached if philosophers gathered together at a convention to take a vote? If they voted yes, would God exist from that moment? Or would God be there even if they voted no?

Will God suddenly come into being when human beings discover Him, or has He always existed? Philosophers try to prove or disprove God through logic, but God is so big that He doesn't fit into human logic too well. Can you show me

1

your mind and explain it to me? If you could grasp your mind 100 percent then you could create your mind, but you cannot do that because you don't know your mind totally. This shows the greatness of your mind. Human beings have a mysterious aspect, and human logic can never perceive the greatness of God or human existence.

This is a very important statement; if you could prove God's existence through logic then God would be small enough to fit into human logic, meaning that human beings could create God and know all about Him. Religious people are much wiser; they have already made up their minds that there is a God, and not only that He existed from the very beginning, but that He will exist throughout eternity.

God created all things, but in all His creation humanity occupies the supreme and central position. It is therefore very important for us to have a clear understanding of the relationship between ourselves and God. Historically, there have been many theories concerning this relationship. Varying opinions, theological concepts and academic schools abound, but the true, living relationship between God and human beings remains an unsettled question.

Because the relationship between God and ourselves is so fundamental to life, our understanding cannot proceed until we have clarified this question thoroughly. Although various religions have developed through human history, there must be one principle common to all religions which can clarify the relationship between God and ourselves. God wants us to understand this principle in its ultimate sense, and through His revelation to our hearts today, this understanding is possible. If there is a God, He definitely needs human beings, and He will do everything possible to develop this relationship .

To begin our discussion, let me ask you the question, "What is the most precious thing in your life?" What will you answer? Some might say, "Power." Some would undoubtedly say money: "Money is everything." And others would suggest, "Wisdom or knowledge." Then, are those elements—power, money, knowledge—the most important things in life? When we look into this question deeply, other thoughts emerge. We soon come to the conclusion that the most precious thing is love; love is the most precious thing in life. And second to love, life itself is most precious. If we have love and life, we need one thing further—an ideal. These three elements—love, life, and an ideal—are not just precious and profound in value, they are the very things that make our lives worth living.

All people long for eternal life; so too we feel an innate desire for our love and ideals to be eternal, unchanging, unique, and everlasting. Many writers in history have described the beauty of eternal love. What writer has ever felt moved to glorify the love that changes night and day? The many religions of the world which testify to a life beyond this earthly one testify to the reality of our desire for eternity.

Furthermore, "love" and "ideals" are empty and without meaning by themselves, in isolation. Love exists only when there is someone to love and someone to be loved by. An ideal needs to be shared with someone. Love and ideals come alive as soon as they are manifested in a reciprocal and complementary relationship of give and take established between a subject and an object. We are in the position of the object and always need someone to be in the subject position. Love and ideals will bud and blossom into full flower only when two elements are in a subject-object relationship. Thus, those things which are of supreme importance in human life come about only through relationships.

Are human beings the cause, the source of the universe, or did someone create us? How can we be the cause of the universe when we did not even create ourselves? It is obvious that we are resultant beings. We are the products of some cause. Therefore, a subject or cause must exist. There must be a cause for the existence of human beings. This subject, or cause, then, is the essential reality. We should be as certain of this as we are of our own existence. Whatever name you choose for that cause doesn't matter. The most important thing is that He is there. And we call him, "God."

Let us put our question to God. "What is the most precious thing to you, God?" God will answer, "Love, life, and my ideal are the most precious things to me." Does God need money? He created all things. Everything belongs to Him anyway. He does not need money. Does God need power? He is already the Source of all power. What about knowledge? God is omniscient and the Source of all knowledge. Yes, God is all these things; but can He have love, life, and His ideal all by Himself? He wants to share, to have give and take with someone in a reciprocal relationship. Even almighty God cannot experience the values of love, life, and His ideal when He is alone. That is why God created His object, His image, man and woman.

Now I shall ask, "Why do we human beings act the way we do?" The answer is simple: Because God acts that way. All human traits originate in God. Why are we the way we are? Because God is the way He is. This is the meaning of our being created in the image of God.

We are mirrors reflecting the characteristics of God. God is just like you and me. God is the Origin. Therefore, our love comes from the love of God. Our life comes from the life of God, and our ideals come from the ideal of God. We feel these are the most precious things because God first felt these things were most precious. God is the Subject of love, the Subject of life, and the Subject of ideals. We are the objects of love, the objects of life, and the objects of ideals. Therefore, if God is absolute, we are to be absolute. If God is unchanging, we are to be unchanging. If God is unique, we are to be unique. If God is everlasting, we are to be everlasting. Our eternal life is not just a fantasy. It is reality. Since God is eternal, His objects, men and women, must be created for eternity. Otherwise, we cannot reflect the nature of our eternal God.

If there is a God of love, life, and ideals, and that God does not manifest all these qualities in human beings, His object, then God has defeated His very purpose of creating.

God either projected the full value of Himself in His object, or He created nothing at all. God is the Subject to man and woman, and we are the objects to God. The object is the full reflection of the subject. So man and woman together are the visible form of God, and God is the invisible form of man and woman. Subject and object are one. God and human being are one. Human being is incarnate God. If not, we would not be able to reflect fully God's image. God could not realize His joy, the purpose of His creation. When we as objects are not as perfect as God Himself is perfect, we cannot reflect fully the love, life, and ideal of God. So man and woman, the object of God, is as important in value as God Himself.

In the same way that our own minds are real to us, God would have been a living reality to us. Your mind dictates your actions, and the relationship between God and human beings should have been the same. In our present state we must be careful of our words before we speak, but what about a perfected person? A perfected person is automatically a reflection of the universal mind, that is, God. No one of perfection would be able to deny God. In addition, the dignity and integrity of true original parents, of true Adam and Eve, would remain for thousands of years, so that all their descendants would maintain the same dignity and integrity as persons that Adam and Eve enjoyed.

The relationship between God and humanity would have been of perfect oneness; God and people would have walked together for eternity. You cannot separate yourself from your own mind, and in the same way men and women would have been unable to separate themselves from God. That would have been human perfection. If there had been no fall and that perfection had prevailed, such people would have become the nucleus of the universe.

The perfected home would have become a unit or model for the heavenly society, nation and world, such that no matter how far the human world expanded, it would always resemble one human being. Then who should be the center of the universe? Actually the central axis of the universe is formed by God and Adam and Eve. Why would God need Adam and Eve? Why do they need Him? For two purposes.

First of all, God's ideal of love would be fulfilled through Adam and Eve. Second, and this is very important, the incorporeal God would have been made visible through men and women. In other words, Adam and Eve were supposed to be the visible form of God, and through them the invisible God could have made a relationship with the visible, physical world. God's ultimate purpose for the creation of Adam and Eve is this: After being perfected here on earth in oneness with God, Adam and Eve would have passed away into spirit world. There Adam and Eve's own spirit selves would be like the body of God, and inside them God would be dwelling as their minds; God Himself would be the mind of Adam and Eve.

Today we have our mind and body, with an inseparable relationship between the two. Similarly, when Adam and Eve were perfected here on earth and then were elevated to the spirit world, God would have been the mind of Adam and Eve and they would have been the spirit body of God, so that God and people in spirit world would have been inseparable, one body. In this world people speak about dying, but actually there is no such thing as death. Instead of dying you just pass into a new realm after giving up your physical body. Your spirit self becomes your body in the spirit world, and God will become the center of that body as the mind of your spirit self.

I want to illustrate the value of relationship, even for God. If I made vigorous gestures and shouted, but without directing such gestures and shouts to anyone else, I am sure that anyone who saw me would wonder, "Is that man crazy?" But if I have someone to have give and take with, some object out there to respond to me—even one small child in front of me—and I pour out my heart and soul to that person, then I am considered normal. The sole difference is the presence of someone as object.

Thus we can understand the value of an object with

which to share relationship. The object in fact through full relationship comes to have value equal to that of the subject. As we are the objects to God, He has placed us in a position equal to Himself. Thus, human beings share the same value as God and are just as important as God. Even though God is most high and noble and mighty, He too must have His object. Can He otherwise feel joy? Joy comes when you receive stimulation from the object. Not even God can be joyful alone. I hope you see my earlier point, that if there is a God, He must need human beings. You must realize that God created human beings and the universe for joy. But God's joy remains dormant until He can have full give and take with us.

So far in Christianity, many churches placed God so high up in heaven, and pushed humanity so low in hell, that there has been an uncrossable gap between us and God. A wide and raging river has separated humanity from God. People have not dared to reach out to God as a living Reality. We have been unable to realize that God is so close, so real, so approachable, that we can even dwell with Him. St. Paul taught that we are supposed to be the living temples of God. Yet conventional Christianity has been unable to make that a reality.

No matter how wealthy and famous you may be, unless you have someone with whom to have give and take so that you can share your joy, your sorrow, your opinions, and your ideals, you are just a poor man or woman. We feel joy and sadness because God's heart can feel joy and sadness. Not until this time in history did we ever believe that God could feel sorrow. And God can feel excitement or indignation, just as we can. We, the objects of God, have this ability to experience emotion because our Subject, God, has the same capacity for emotion. God is the first Personality, and human personality comes from God. How then can we become true objects to God? By our efforts and hard work alone? No. There is but one way to come together in oneness with God. That way is through love—oneness in love with God.

Let me illustrate. Suppose there is a famous man. Opposite him is a woman who is unassuming and meek and without beauty or education. However, once this great man and this humble woman establish a circuit of give and take in love, she will instantly achieve his level of prestige. Let's say the man's name is Jones and he falls in love with this woman and marries her. She then becomes Mrs. Jones and returns his love with all her heart. Whatever power, authority and prestige Mr. Jones enjoys, Mrs. Jones would share in every respect. Now, what does this teach us? Once we have a relationship of love with God and become one with Him, our value increases instantly to the level of God's value. This is the value that Jesus has—divine value. And such love as this is everlasting, unchanging, and unique.

Today is the time when we must fulfill this fundamental relationship between God and ourselves. The subject and object must be one just as cause and effect are one. The Bible says, "I am the Alpha and the Omega, the first and the last, the beginning and the end." (Rev. 22:13) Within God, two are one. He is the beginning and we are the end. He is the first and we are the last. And the relationship between God and human beings is a circuit because beginning and end come together in oneness.

Peace, happiness and joy are the fruits of harmony in love. Therefore, in God's ideal of creation, He planned the relationship between Himself and us to be lived with harmony in love, with harmony in life, and with harmony in ideal.

I have stated that God is Subject and we are the objects and that the object is just as important as the subject. We now want to know precisely what our position as God's object means.

When God created man and woman He gave them wisdom and ambition. Wisdom gives us the power to compare, and ambition gives us the desire to strive for the best. If there are two choices before us, A and B, we will automatically compare them to determine which is better. Our human desire leads us to choose, and our ambition does not let us rest until we have obtained ultimate fulfillment.

Let me employ another analogy for illustration. Let's say there is a most handsome man. He is not only handsome, but all-powerful and all-wise. You would have the ambition to have some kind of personal relationship with this great man. What would you want it to be? Would you like to be just his servant? No, in your heart you know there is a position better than that of servant. Would you like to be only his friend? No, you would still not be happy. Would you like to be only his adopted son or daughter? Will this position bring you complete happiness? No, I don't think so. You would still crave some closer position. But there is one relationship beyond which there is nothing more intimate. That is to become a true son or daughter of this man. With this relationship you will have reached the ultimate fulfillment and you cannot have ambition for anything more.

Why, then, do we have the ambition to become true sons and daughters? Because that is the position in which to receive love most fully. There is no closer or deeper relationship in human society than that between the parent and child. Once you have your parents' love, you possess everything they have. Every joy of the parent, all the power of the parent, all skill and wisdom and ambition and desire of the parent—all will then be yours. In receiving the love of a parent there is no procedure, no paperwork or ceremony necessary to grant those things to a child. The parent and child are automatically one. This principle is expressed in human families, and it applies as well between us and God.

Then, what kind of relationship would you like to have with God? Would you be content just to be His servant? Or would you prefer to be His friend? Would you rather be His adopted child, or would you like to find a way to become God's own true child? I know you will be satisfied with nothing short of the ultimate position as sons and daughters of God.

God's ultimate purpose in His creation of human beings is to give to us all His love, all His life, and all His ideal. You are to occupy the entire love of God, to the depth of His heart. By becoming His true sons and daughters, your desire will be fulfilled. That is your ultimate destiny. Then you will be saturated with the love of God. You will be filled with joy and feel overwhelmed by a total satisfaction in life.

There is no limit to joy. Happiness has no end. When you are standing in the love of God, every cell in your body jumps for joy. You breathe in and out with the entire universe. In this state your life is fulfilled. This is how God means us to live, intoxicated in love and joy. And through our joy, God receives His joy. The joy of human beings is the joy of God; the joy of God is the joy of human beings.

If humankind could have been one with God as our Father, abiding with Him, living with Him in the greatest love, how happy we would have been! And on God's part, how happy He would have been to live with His true children. Being the highest in every sense, He would have been overjoyed with happiness! He would have lived with us in the greatest love. Have you ever stopped to imagine how hilariously He would have laughed and danced and rejoiced to see us and to live with us? It is our great remorse not to have been able to live with such a Father, from whom every joy, every happiness, every dance, everything good and happy begins. Everything good would have started from God. But we have never seen, never experienced goodness to such a full and complete extent.

Early in my life God called me for a mission as His instrument. I was called to reveal His truth for Him, as His prophet. I committed myself unyieldingly in pursuit of truth, searching the hills and valleys of the spiritual world. The time suddenly came to me when heaven opened up, and I was privileged to communicate with Jesus Christ and the living God directly. Since then I have received many astonishing revelations. God Himself told me that the most basic and central truth of this universe is that *God is the*

Father and we are His children. We are all created as children of God. And He said there is nothing closer, nothing deeper, nothing more intimate than when Father and child are one: One in love, one in life, and one in ideal.

Love, life, and ideal are at the central point where father and child meet. Once we unite there, then God's love is our love; God's ideal is our ideal; God's life is our life. And there is no other relationship where you can have unity of life, unity of love, and unity of ideal any more than in the parent-child relationship. This is a fundamental reality of the universe.

How do we come into being in this world? The father and mother become one through their love, and bring together their lives and ideals. Their love precedes our birth. Love is the force which unites. Husband and wife become one in love. This means the husband's love, life, and ideal become the wife's, and the wife's love, life, and ideal become the husband's. This is the way that two live as one, and two become one flesh. Upon this foundation of oneness in love, a new life can be generated.

When a child is born, that child is the manifestation of his or her parents' love, life, and ideal. When you look at your own child, you are actually seeing another you. You are looking at the fruit of your love, the fruit of your life, and the fruit of your ideal. You are looking at your second self—another visible form of yourself.

Now let us expand this truth onto a universal scale. God created men and women as His sons and daughters. He wants to see Himself in human beings. Therefore, the Bible says, ". . . God created man in his own image, in the image of God he created him; male and female he created them." (Gen. 1:27)

Human beings are created in the likeness of God. In other words, God made Himself incarnate in human beings. We are the mirror of the living God, and His every virtue, characteristic, and quality is reflected in this mirror. God surely wants men and women to reflect His love, life, and ideal. Human life is the fruit of God's love, life, and ideal.

God desired to substantiate Himself in the world, and He finally approached that point with the birth of the original parents, Adam and Eve. God is the Father of Adam and Eve, and naturally He must have some resemblance to them. It was a moment of great revolution for God Himself when He finally came to encounter Himself in His children, substantially in the flesh. Naturally it was a romantic, exciting moment when God saw Adam and Eve!

The morning of glory for God in the creation of the entire universe was the moment of Adam and Eve's birth. When you ask what God looks like, the answer is that God is like Adam and Eve. Before Adam and Eve fell they were the walking, physical God here on earth. As the visible form of God, they were to take over Lordship of the physical world, whereas God remained the invisible Lord of the entire spirit world.

You may ask an important question: Why did God create human beings? God wanted to assume tangible form and the day Adam and Eve were born was almost like the day of God's own birth. As Adam and Eve grew to completion, God spiritually grew into a greater fulfillment together with them. God and His children were one and the same person actually, and therefore when Adam or Eve laughed, God laughed. When they were moody then God was also moody. When they worked, God worked.

Why should it be like that? Everything is geared toward fulfillment, both here on earth and in heaven, with God and human beings growing together. The growth of men and women is the growth of God Himself as well. We talk about perfection, but what is it? Perfection means the perfection of love, with no lack of any kind, a perfectly round love.

Do you know there is love because you have seen it? We do not see love, but we know it is there. Do you handle love or does love handle and embrace you? The latter is true. Love can say, "You are mine," but you cannot say, "Love is mine." Love doesn't belong to anyone; love belongs to all. Suppose there were a terrible dictator who wanted to conquer love all for himself. No matter what that dictator might say, love would laugh at him because it will never come under the control of one person. Could Eastern and Western people be brought into unity by military power, or by the power of culture and religion? One unique power can unite them—love.

How wonderful, how simply wonderful it is to live this perfected life of God! This is the true life of joy, unequalled by any earthly joy. Once you reach this state of perfection you don't need prayer. Why should you? You meet God face to face, and you live heart to heart with Him. You converse with God. You no longer need religion, and you don't need a savior. All these things of religion are part of the mending process, the process of restoration. A person of perfect health does not need a physician. The person in perfect union with God does not need a savior.

Life in union with God is the one great way to live—life with God, life in God, and God living in you. This was the spiritual state of Jesus when he said, "Do you not believe that I am in the Father and the Father in me? . . ." (John 14:10) God and human beings will embrace in one all-consuming love. This is the state where God is made the living Reality. You no longer *believe*, but you *know*. And you *live* the truth. If you really experience this kind of love and oneness with God, then you have tasted the supreme experience of life. Of the many Christian leaders in America today, how many have had that wonderful experience, receiving the profound love of God?

God made us to live our lives in intoxication. We are meant to be intoxicated by the love of God. Since we lost this original capacity we seek unnatural, artificial intoxication—getting drunk on alcohol, marijuana, or drugs. The perfect man or woman, however, is created to be intoxicated in the love of God. There is nothing that can go beyond this feeling of joy. Every cell in your body will explode with joy. Your eyes and ears, the tissues in your face, your arms and legs—everything will be newly alive in a rapture of joy. Nothing else can ever match this quality of joy. Once a person discovers the way to be intoxicated in the love of God, even though you urge him or her to try drugs, alcohol or whatever, they would refuse. Those things are flat compared to the taste of the love of God. The love of God is precisely like electricity, which can be conducted by any part of the body. If the love of God touches your mind, your mind will jump. If it touches your emotions, they will jump. If it touches your ears or your eyes, they will jump.

Have you really experienced God's love that vividly? Feeling the love of God is similar to receiving an electric shock; when it hits a person he or she may appear unconscious but inside they are actually trembling with ecstatic joy. Once you feel the living, active love of God you want to close your eyes, but your eyes cannot close. Your whole body is so activated that you cannot stop reacting to that love. God is almighty and can do anything, so certainly He wants everyone to be part of such an explosive, gigantic, dramatic love, not love which is flat and pale-tasting like three-day-old beer.

Put yourself in the position of God. You are capable of doing anything. You want to create love of such magnitude that when it moves the entire universe will be excited, not listless. When God laughs He wants to have the entire universe laugh in the joy of love. Such a joyful love cannot be created by selfish people. When you totally release yourself in giving, you can taste such love; that's God's love. This is the plan of God's original creation. When you say, "Heavenly Father," do you really have a living and vibrant feelings of God's presence? Don't you want to hear God answering, "Yes, my child?"

Here is my gift to you tonight: I want you to realize that the true relationship between God and human beings is a subject and object relationship. You are His sons and His daughters. Once you have achieved unity with God, nothing can trouble you. Neither sorrow nor loneliness, sickness or anything else under the sun can discourage you. God is the ultimate security. You could pay many millions of dollars and still not buy that kind of security. It is priceless. No money can buy it. This is the *total experience* of life. We are meant to live with God.

Once you become such men and women you will be the center of the universe wherever you go, whether to Mars or to the moon, to the spirit world or physical world. No matter how small a portion you may occupy in the center, you are still in the image of God. You will fit into any place in the universe and be accepted.

Your life is therefore the most valuable thing in this universe. That is why Jesus said, "For what will it profit a man, if he gains the whole world and forfeits his life? Or what shall a man give in return for his life?" (Matt. 16:26) Jesus is talking about life with God. Life without God is like a burned-out electric bulb which cannot give out light. A life without God is death.

Jesus Christ is the one man who lived God's ideal in its fullest realization. He was the first man of perfection ever to walk the earth, and he came to restore the true relationship between God and human beings. But after Jesus' crucifixion, Christianity made him into only God. This is why the gap between God and ourselves has never been bridged. Jesus is a man in whom God is incarnate. But he is not God Himself, the Father. It is written in I Timothy 2:5, "For there is one God, and there is one mediator between God and men, the man Christ Jesus, . . ." The dwelling of God within Jesus was a total reality. He said, "Do you not believe that I am in the Father and the Father in me? . . ." (John 14:10). Jesus is, indeed, the only begotten son of God, but God does not want *only* Jesus as His son. All mankind is created to be able to say, "I am in the Father and the Father in me." The entire purpose of Jesus' coming can be summarized in one sentence: Jesus came to bring the resurrection needed so that human love can be perfected to the point where we can come into the direct dominion of God's love. This is the fully attainable goal of everyone.

2
Jesus' Standard
Of Goodness

Our first step in becoming the true sons and daughters of God is to comprehend clearly God's view of good and evil. What is goodness and what is evil?

The eternal standard of good and evil is defined by God. The sharp definition of good and evil existed at the time of His creation, long before evil ever came into being in the Garden of Eden. God's view of good and evil will never change. God is eternal, His law is eternal, and His definition is eternal and unchanging despite the passage of time.

It is common to look upon human self-centeredness as the basis of evil. Let us examine this perception. All of our human traits originate in God. We recognize that there is some human tendency for selfishness. This is natural because at one time God Himself was self-centered. This fact may surprise you, but you must understand that before God created human beings and the universe, He was *all alone,* with no one to care for except Himself. However, the very instant that God initiated creation, His full concept of life emerged. God now lives for His counterpart—not for Himself.

What is creation? Creation means nothing more than the Creator, God, projecting Himself into a substantial form. He made Himself incarnate symbolically in the universe, and He made himself incarnate directly in man and woman. When God takes form, this is creation. God invested Himself in the creation. God's investment of energy, idea and love *is* the creation.

The Bible in the book of Genesis makes creation sound simple and easy. Genesis gives us the impression that God's creation is accomplished through some magic of His words. God simply says, "Let there be a world," and presto!—the world comes into being. Then He says, "Let there be man," and poof!—Adam and Eve come into being.

But now it has been revealed that it was not this easy at all. God invested all of Himself in His creation. He did not reserve even one ounce of power. Creation was His total labor, His total effort of giving all of Himself. When God put His entire heart and soul into the creation of His object, He was investing 100 percent of Himself. Only in this way could He create His second self, the visible God.

Therefore, after His creation God was no longer existing just for Himself. God began existing for His son and daughter, Adam and Eve. He exists to love, He exists to give. God is the totally unselfish existence. God can no longer exist alone. "Love" and "ideal" only take on meaning when partners are in a complementary relationship. God initiated creation and made an investment He cannot lose. When God poured all of His love, life, and ideal into His second self, He had to, in a sense, realize a profit. God knew that when He invested all He had—100 percent—His object would mature and return to Him many, many times over the fruits of His love, life, and ideal. His object, man and woman, is everything to God. The life of the object attracts God. God wants to go and dwell with His object on earth.

Let us look at an illustration. Suppose there is a great artist. If she works at random without feeling, she cannot create anything worthwhile. To create the masterpiece of her lifetime, the artist must put all of her heart and soul into her creation. That is the only way for her to come up with a great work of art. If an artist works in this way, her art becomes her life.

God is the greatest of all artists. When He created His masterpiece, man and woman, He poured His heart into the process. He poured His soul into it. He poured all of His wisdom and all of His effort into it. God wished only to exist for Adam and Eve and all humankind. He saved not a single ounce of effort when He created them. Thus, humanity has become the life of God.

God set the pattern for the universe. In the ideal existence we live for others. The subject exists for the object and the object exists for the subject. God's definition of goodness is total giving, total service, and absolute unselfishness. We are to live our lives for others. You live for others and others live for you. God lives for human beings and we live for God. The husband lives for his wife and the wife lives for her husband. This is goodness. And here unity, harmony, and prosperity abound.

I want you to know that love is the most holy and supreme impulse. If you can lay down your life for the sake of your spouse, you are the greatest lover. Likewise, those parents who give their lives for their children have the highest love.

We must learn the lessons of love from nature. The holiest people have always been on intimate terms with nature. You should naturally want to go out every day and look at the sky and the birds and the animals in order to perceive new lessons in love. Your home must be one of love, not only for your family but also for the things of nature. All the creatures, including the insects, will want to become a part of your "love orchestra." You will have plants, animals, flowers and insects dwelling together in love.

The universe welcomes those men and women who consider love the supreme value. Does anyone here think I am wrong in saying this? Love is almighty; it is greater than life itself. There are no adjectives large enough to describe love. It is absolute, it is unchanging, it is beautiful, it is sweet; yet none of these words encompass love. Throughout the history of literature and poetry, what is more praised— love or life? Or maybe power and money are the focus of poetry? No, love is most praised. The reason is very simple, yet perhaps most poets don't fully understand.

You were not born for your own sake but for the sake of others. As long as your terminology is "we" and "us" the universe supports you, but as soon as you think in terms of "I" and "me" the universe will turn against you. Eventually you will be expelled from this universe. Can you complain against this rule?

This is the beauty of marriage—it pushes people to think always of themselves in terms of another. Likewise living in a family requires us to think in terms of "we"—the children think of their parents, the parents think of the children, each child thinks of the other brothers and sisters.

Would you, as a man, be disturbed if I said that you were created for a woman? Perhaps, some of you are proud of your masculinity and would not want to hear this. But this is the principle of God's creation, and you must not be sorry to hear these words. Man lives his life for this partner, not for himself.

Let us assume that you, as a woman, are a beauty queen. No matter how beautiful you are, your beauty is not for your own gratification; it is for the delight of men. We are created to live for each other. This is the very reason for our existence; we exist for others, for an object, for a counterpart. This is the principle for all human relationships in our society. Parents exist for their children, and children exist for their parents. Then both parents and children, when they give unselfishly, become united in a circular motion.

This circling motion is the motion of unity. When you give and take, the give and take action creates a circular motion. Circular motion alone can be eternal, because there you will find no end. Therefore, all of God's creation is based on a pattern of circular movement, since He created for eternity. Even our faces are round, although there is one central vertical line. Our eyeballs are round, and there are upper and lower lips which make up a round mouth. The sun is round, the moon, the earth, and all heavenly bodies are round. They are each rotating on their own axes and revolving around the others. Everything in this universe has complementary give and take action between subject and object. Give and take action occurs between artery and vein, and thus blood circulates through the body. Human sickness is the state where the balance of give and take action is broken, and normal circulating motion is stopped. Without having this give and take action between subject and object, without abiding by this principle, nothing endures for eternity. The universe exists in continual give and take action, turning from the inner to the outer core of existence and back again. The power of the entire universe goes into the tiniest embryo and then the embryo sprouts and gives itself to the entire universe. This is the ultimate form of give and take.

Each individual is a tiny being compared with the size of the universe. However, each individual feels the need to link him or herself with the whole universe. Why do we have that need? There must be a reason for it. It is because the vast universe is truly linked with each tiny life. The universe relates itself with each embryo, each person's origin; then each embryo expands itself to the universe. The universe comes within you; you relate with the universe, like a continually moving spiral from inside to outside. All existence that is based upon God's principle of harmonious give and take is a good existence.

Then, what is evil? Evil is the emergence of selfishness into this world. If an individual takes off in his or her own direction, that person might say, "I just want to exist for myself. This is my universe and it exists for me to indulge myself to the utmost." The more such a person would move, the more destruction he or she would bring to the universe. If enough people followed this example, everything would be destroyed. The order and harmony of the whole world would be ruined by such a "freedom-loving" attitude. God's principle of unselfish giving was twisted into an ungodly principle of selfish taking. The ungodly position of desiring to be served rather than to serve was thereby established.

The source of evil is Satan. He was in the position to serve God, but instead he posed as another god and subjugated man and woman for his own benefit. God is the absolute positive force in the universe. Then Satan posed as another positive force. Two positives naturally repel each other. Satan is a fallen archangel. He left his position as faithful servant to God and God's children, and he challenged and competed with God. *His motivation was selfishness.* Out of his selfishness comes the origin of evil and sin.

What happened is this: Eve fell from her position as God's first daughter, becoming the first victim of Satan and transforming herself into a creature of selfishness. Together Eve and Satan then successfully brought Adam into their selfish world. They committed sin through an illicit, unchaste love relationship. And what was the love relationship between them like? Everything should start from God. Then it goes to Adam and Eve, and then to the Archangel. But things went in a reverse way: first the Archangel, then Eve and Adam.

From the standpoint of the Archangel, both Adam and Eve were in the position of his Master. That means that the Archangel seduced Eve, the Master's intended wife. After that shame Eve wanted to justify her sin, and she tempted Adam by having Adam commit the same sin. All of them defied God. If you were in the place of God, what would you do? Can you simply forgive them? Well, can we say that God just does things at random—without reference to law or principle? We say God is absolute, but is this in the sense that He can forgive them in a way which might be evil? We know that God is an absolute being only in the ways which are good.

God's original intention in creating Adam and Eve, the Archangel, and the whole creation has been nullified. But God cannot cut them off and tread down upon them. God was the Master and Creator of all those people and things; thus, the sin was committed within His family. So it was natural for God to grieve over what took place. He was in shame, too. In your own family, if you commit sins, or if your mother commits a sin, would your father be honored or put to shame? Then how grieved would God have been having that kind of son and daughter and that kind of a servant? He was remorseful, grieved and angered. In light of all this we can say that God is a grieving God and an ashamed God. He is a God who has tasted the bitterness of sin. If your son or daughter is sinful, you feel that you are the sinner.

By this tragic event, God was isolated by man and woman in the Garden of Eden. This is the meaning of the Genesis account of the fall. Human history started on the wrong footing, without God. The foundation for the evil history of the human race was laid, and Satan was established as the ruler of this world. We must understand clearly what Satan did. Satan stole and destroyed the very element that God was seeking to perfect with man and woman: His love. The loving relationship between God and His children was ripped apart. Selfishness came into being at the beginning of human history, and now our world is rampant with killing, lying, and stealing. All of these actions in the evil world are motivated by selfishness.

Evil subjugates others for its own benefit, while good sacrifices itself for the benefit of others. Since the human fall, God's work has been the restoration of original goodness. God wants to abolish the world of evil and recreate the world of goodness. We have lost our health. We have become sick people. The salvation of God is, therefore, the restoration of human beings to a healthy state once again. This world, being the kingdom of hell on earth, is a place where a savior is necessary.

When human beings consummate their life in hell on earth, upon being elevated into spirit world they can have no other destination than hell. Let me give an analogy. In the autumn beautiful apples are harvested, but if a particular apple is rotten then the farmer throws it away. There is no other place for it. Those people who end up in hell are human trash in God's sight. One apple may have bad skin, yet be very good on the inside, while another apple may look good on the surface, yet be rotten inside and worthless. Human beings belong in the second category. There is no possibility for a fallen person who is corrupted on the inside to be easily salvaged.

Even though there may be some damage on an apple's surface, if its seeds are intact then it still has value. However, human beings are the opposite, being intact on the outside, but rotten on the inside. After the fall human beings became rotten to the core.

God sowed the seed of goodness, but before He could gather its fruit, Satan invaded with his evil seed and harvested his evil fruit. For this reason, God must sow the seed of goodness once again. To do this job God needs certain tools. The religions of the world have served as these tools for God. Throughout history, good religions have taught God's way of life, centered upon sacrificial love and duty. Thus Christianity may be considered the most advanced and progressive religion because it teaches this sacrificial love and duty in supreme form.

In history there are many teachings. One is that if someone mistreats you, repay him in the same way: an eye for an eye, a tooth for a tooth, a death for a death. However, the most revolutionary teaching was given by the one who said, "Love your enemy and pray for those who persecute you." Needless to say, that was Jesus Christ.

Did Jesus make his own proclamations, or was he teaching according to someone else's will, denying his own ego? What do you think? Jesus was not proclaiming his own message. Above him was God. Jesus' teaching was God's teaching; his emotional reaction to things was not his own. This means that the proclamations which Jesus made were God's, and God can be trusted 100 percent.

Ultimately speaking, we can conclude that in this universe there is only one being you can fully trust: God; and His characteristics were manifested through Jesus Christ.

Jesus came as a savior, but his teaching was, ". . . the Son of man came not to be served but to serve . . ." (Matt. 20:28) Jesus taught that the greatest love in this universe is to give one's life for one's enemy. The teaching of the Bible is contrary to the common rule of our worldly society. It is exactly the opposite of the way of this self-centered world. The Bible teaches complete giving and total sacrifice. "He who finds his life will lose it, and he who loses his life for my sake will find it." (Matt. 10:39) It seems almost foolish to think seriously about living this way in our evil society. But once you know God's principle, you discover that there is actually no wisdom greater than this.

Jesus Christ's teachings hit the very core of this fundamental truth. The more you give the more you receive. God rewards total giving with total love, and total sacrifice with total life. Giving creates room for God's love to enter. The more room and the greater the vacuum created by your giving, the faster you will be filled by the flow of God's love.

To be treated well you must first treat others well. You reap as you sow. Sow evil to reap evil; sow goodness to reap goodness. Your concern should be how to give, and how to give well. As for the return to you, you must trust in God. He will take care of it. We all have only one lifetime; at the end of your life, the serious question you must answer will be how well did you actually love God. The question has already been raised by Jesus, as recorded in the Bible. He demanded of people that they love him more than their own spouses or children or anyone else.

Love is of all different qualities. What is the standard for loving which we must be able to meet before we are actually qualified to say to someone, "I love you"? You must know where you are in relation to that standard. Jesus' standard of loving went beyond everything in a person's life: loved ones and precious belongings—everything. Each person has a claim on his or her own environment, family, country and world. All of that had to be abandoned, if necessary, in order to love Jesus; this was the clear-cut standard which the Bible records.

Perhaps you think about these things and you pray with that attitude, but the true test is in how you live your life. Let us take an illustration of a good man and a bad man. Let us say there is one man who has ten friends. Day in and day out this man is unselfishly serving his ten friends. People cannot help but love this man. He can become the very best friend to ten people. Then his influence will spread to the relatives and friends of those first ten people. By giving and serving unselfishly this man becomes prosperous. He is a center of harmony and unity because he lives God's principle. Unselfishness brings prosperity. Here is a good man.

But suppose, on the contrary, this man said to his friends, "You ten, bring everything to me; you are here to serve me." Before he spoke this way to his friends three times, everyone would end all connection with him. Soon he would be left all alone. Isn't that true, even in our society? It is universally true: A self-centered doctrine, a self-centered philosophy, a self-centered way of life will fling you head over heels down the tragic road of self-destruction. But if you will live your life in service to others, you will find prosperity. It may seem that such a route would lead you to ruin, but it will not. The only reason it may not always bring prosperity to you is because you do not give to the very end. In the middle you suddenly become skeptical. You change your heart or pity yourself and thus shrink from God's law of total giving. The good result never materializes. Total giving is the way of prosperity because it is the way of God.

If any individual sacrifices himself or herself for another individual, that individual becomes a hero to others. If one family is sacrificial for the well-being of another family, then that family becomes a heroic family among all families. Peoples and nations who sacrifice themselves for the benefit of others become champions of nations. A man who gives his life for his parents is a pious son. A man who gives his life for his nation is a patriot. And a man who gives his life for all humankind is a saint.

It is not God's way to have the individual going in one direction, the family going another way, and the nation and world going yet another. The true way of life starts with the individual but then continues through to the universal level. We have to go through several stages, including the spiritual world. There is always a test to pass at each level before you can advance further. Who is testing you? It is not God but Satan and the satanic world who test you. Satan is in the position of prosecutor while God is in the position of judge and you are the defendant. Jesus Christ is your advocate. There is a court of judgement on every level of your advancement and finally God, the universal sovereign, has His own court. No one can escape from defending him or herself there.

Christians preach about loving one's enemies, but Jesus also said to love your neighbor. Who is a Christian's near neighbor? Certainly it is another Christian. But are they doing it? Do Catholics love Mormons? Do Jehovah's Witnesses love Methodists? It doesn't matter who calls us heretics; whoever practices this principle of loving one's enemy is closer to God and is the orthodox Christian. That is my belief. Love can unite. If Christians practice love then we can unite with Christians and the Christians can unite all the religions of the world.

Are Moonies heretics or not? How do you know? If you tell the Christians of the world what Unification Church is about, they may say you are a heretic. The important thing is to inherit the true tradition and spirit of Christianity, however, and as long as we inherit that doctrine and practice it, we are the most orthodox.

Even though Christians themselves have violated many

of God's laws they still judge others, calling them heretics or anti-Christs. Some Christians insist that the Unification Church is false and heretical, but are they qualified to pass judgement? Did God give them that authority? If Christians are only concerned about their own church denomination, they shall be judged by the people who live beyond the circumference of their own religion, the people who totally dedicate themselves for the sake of God.

Jesus Christ proclaimed this very truth. He strove for the fulfillment of God's truth on earth. He came not to satisfy his nation's selfish purpose, but to achieve salvation for the entire world.

God intended the chosen nation of Israel to serve as the prepared instrument of the Messiah for his mission of world salvation. The nation of Israel did not know this. Some people conceived of the coming Messiah as a military leader who would restore the political empire of King David for the glory of the Jews. How wrong they were!

We may think that God is interested in just one particular family or nation. Up to the present moment, when the usual Christian prays hard, leading a godly life, he or she is working for individual salvation, or at most the salvation of his or her family. We are used to doing that much, but not beyond that. We have not realized that if we really struggle to set up a nation under God's truth, our families and we ourselves will be included in that scope. By setting eyes on broader things, those smaller areas are already saved or included. Today Christianity is declining, and that is the cause. And if Christianity as a whole declines, even the family and the individual will be lost. Many Christians believe that when the Lord comes the second time, he will be here just for themselves and their own family. Does any Christian realize that when the Lord comes again he will establish a whole nation of God's choice, as a base from which he will restore the world? Is there any single Christian in the whole world who strongly believes that when Christ comes again there must be a national foundation established for him to work on? If you are asked what would you want to save, you should immediately answer, not yourself, but at least a nation. Because you know that, if you could save a whole nation, your family would be included there and so would you. So you and your family would also be saved.

If you recall, in the days of Jesus Christ the same was true. Some people of that time thought that God had prepared 4,000 years of history to send Jesus to the Jewish people in order to save that nation. They thought and desired that when Jesus came, he would take revenge on their enemies. They would be the leading nation of the world and all others would come to their knees in front of them. But, if you were in God's position, would you want to save the whole world, save one nation or just one individual? The answer is clear.

Now, why has Christianity spread all over the world? Because Jesus' sacrificial spirit is the mind of the providence, and that is the basic spirit of God's providence—that is, to make yourself a sacrifice for other people. Christianity has received much persecution, but the more it received persecution, the more it prospered. Jesus did not leave any ideology like Marxism, but by the spirit alone he made such great effects in the world. That is done not only by Jesus, but by God's providence and by the cooperation and the will of God Himself. Therefore, the most important thing is: one nation that sacrifices all things for the whole world and all humankind. From that nation will come out a system developed from Jesus himself. The future ideal world will be developed. That nation is sacrificing itself and its sovereignty for the benefit of the whole world. There is no such nation on the earth.

The United States is far away from this position. The individual and individualism are good, but America and Westerners put too much stress on these two things. As a result, they have lost their nation, their people, their family, their parents, and even themselves. They are like hawks and blow where the wind blows.

God's ultimate purpose is not the salvation of any particular individual, church, or nation. God's purpose is to save the whole world. Therefore, the true church would give itself as a sacrifice for the benefit of the world. God sacrificed His son Jesus Christ to save humanity; God's only begotten son was killed as a sacrifice to save humanity. Would it be right or wrong if it were necessary to sacrifice the Unification Church to save America and the rest of the world? People of the world are dying and desperately suffering. If they are your brothers and sisters then you have to reach them and cry out for them. True Christians must be willing to sacrifice their own lives for the salvation of the world and all humankind. However, much Christian teaching today is self-centered. Many Christians are seeking their own personal salvation; they are crying out for "my salvation" and "my heaven." This is contrary to God's truth and contrary to God's ideal. We must steadfastly give, love, sacrifice, and live for the sake of others.

Can we find such a nation on this earth? There is no such nation sacrificing itself. Therefore, religion must sacrifice itself. Religion must sacrifice itself for a nation, and that nation must sacrifice itself for the sake of the world. And the world must sacrifice itself for the sake of God. That way God's ideal of one world can be reached. If this religion is in America, then it must sacrifice all that it has to save America. That religion should not fight to multiply its churches but should work to save the nation, sacrificing its own churches. If it works with such spirit, then that nation will come to that religion and eventually unite with it. And when this religion unites with its nation, they must go forward to save the whole world, sacrificing themselves. Therefore, without sacrifice, God's will cannot be realized.

We are in the position to have to liberate God's heart, which has been very grievous over the human fall. Due to the fall, His happiness has been under bondage, so we have to liberate Him and release Him from grief, relieve Him. Without knowing this fact, Christians or members of any other religion have been asking God to liberate them and do this and that for them without having the notion of our having to liberate God instead.

The Unification Church was created on this earth with that mission, to liberate God's heart. The most important question or problem is how to relieve His heart by restoring ourselves on the individual level, family level, nationwide level, and worldwide level. What God wants is not the world as it is, not Christianity as it is. He wants the world and Christianity and His people to liberate His heart, knowing the fact that His heart is bound in grief, or by sorrow. How many Christians have there been who thought of that? Has there ever been such a nation of God's choice where people have been thinking of liberating God's heart from sorrow?

We must all work for the ideal way of life. I exist for my family, my family exists for our society, our society exists for our nation, our nation exists for the world, all the world exists for God, and God exists for you and me, for all humankind. In this great circle of give and take there is harmony, there is unity, and there is an eternal process of increasing prosperity. Furthermore, since in this circuit all existence will fulfill its purpose of creation, there is abundant and profound joy. This is the kingdom of heaven, in which feelings of happiness overflow.

In our world, selfishness ruins everything. Selfishness in the family causes disharmony, which then erupts into bitterness and strife. Everyone wants to be served instead of serving others. Wives tell their husbands what to do and then seek to be served. Husbands want to be served by their wives. Parents expect service from their children and the children take their parents for granted. This is demonstrated in our families, in our societies, and in our nations.

If human beings loved each other, they would not have wanted to be separated from each other; they would have wanted to come closer and cuddle together and talk together; wherever they went they would want to associate and go back and forth and they could not have forgotten their own language. But, if disharmony exists, if you quarrel, you don't want to be with the opponent; you want to go this way if he wants to go that way and you would never want to eat whatever was made by your opponent. Disharmony was caused by the fall.

In this world today the nations are existing solely for their own national interests. They plot, connive, cheat, and lie. They destroy other nations for their own national benefit. Is there even one nation on earth which pledges to God, "God, you may use this nation as your sacrifice and as your altar, if that is the way you can save the world?" Tell me, where is such a nation? Where?

It is a recognized fact that when America demonstrated the spirit of service and sacrificial duty in the world, and went out of her way to help others in their need—when America gave lives, money, and a helping hand—she enjoyed a golden age. But now America has a selfish attitude. The domestic problems today are very severe. America is at a critical turning point. Today there is deepening division, increasing corruption, and more and more flagrant immorality choking this land.

I am not saying these things just to be critical of America. I am proclaiming the heavenly truth which Jesus brought 2,000 years ago.

I started the Unification Church. If the Unification Church exists solely for the benefit or the welfare of the Unification Church itself, then it is doomed to perish. I founded the Church so that I could give my life, my heart, and my soul for the advancement of the salvation of the world. I teach the members of this Church to have as their only motivation the desire to serve others, to save this nation and the world.

Not all religions are good. There are God-centered religions and Satan-centered religions. How can we distinguish between the two? We can distinguish by observing their actions. Those religions which are trying to take the stronger position and conquer the weak are the evil religions. The good religions always take the lower position and try to sacrifice and serve. A nation's religion should inspire it to work for the sake of the world, not for itself alone. A good religion tries to promote the spirit of service throughout the world.

Jesus did not teach his disciples laws of retaliation. He told them, ". . . if anyone strikes you on the right cheek, turn to him the other also; . . . and if anyone forces you to go one mile, go with him two miles." (Matt. 5:39, 41) You never have to retaliate; all you have to do is completely and totally give, and then God will return to you more and more abundantly.

The greatest puzzle in history is how the name of Jesus, that unknown, uneducated son of a carpenter, became known in every household in the last 2,000 years. Jesus was not well-accepted during his lifetime. He didn't have any formal education and he looked very humble and shabby. He collected friends like fishermen from around the sea of Galilee and tax collectors and harlots. When Jesus went from village to village with such people, saying shocking and unheard of things, the people thought he was crazy and dangerous. He was finally crucified on the cross.

How could the name of such a man become universally known in 2,000 years? Jesus lived according to God's formula. He is a universal man in this respect and this is what sets him apart. He was totally and absolutely a public person who embraced the universe. That is precisely how God has been living through all of history. The philosophies of God and Jesus were absolutely parallel, and after Jesus' death God raised his name up universally.

When Jesus was crucified, Roman soldiers pierced him. And Jesus prayed for his enemies: "Father, forgive them; for they know not what they do." (Luke 23:34) Even at the moment of death on the cross, Jesus was so earnest in forgiving. His very last act was motivated by his love for his enemies. His compassionate mind could embrace not only his own people but also his people's own enemies. He was the supreme form of giving—a paragon of love. He was not just praying for that one Roman soldier who was piercing his side; he was praying for the forgiveness of the entire Roman Empire. He came with a universal, international mission, not for just one soul or one group. Today many Christians are looking for "my Heaven, my little cubbyhole upstairs," but that is not the way God sees it. Either you win the whole world or nothing can be won.

Those who sacrifice themselves for the sake of all humanity can be called true men and women. Jesus was the man who sacrificed himself for humanity. Jesus was the first one who was awakened to the fact that he had to die for the sake of God, God's nation and all of God's peoples. Therefore, people admire Jesus, and God loves him. Both God's love and true human love were revealed through Jesus. A new world made its start through Jesus. The example of Jesus Christ is the absolute standard for all humankind. Just imagine an entire nation composed of Jesus-like men and women. What would you call it? The Kingdom of Heaven on earth—it could be nothing less.

Jesus Christ was Lord over all life because of his unparalleled form of loving, giving, and sacrifice. He will remain Lord forever. In the same way, no one in this universe surpasses the total giving and loving of God. So God is God forever. He reigns over all creation.

Look at the decline of Rome. The entire Roman Empire collapsed in front of the army with no weapons, the army of Jesus Christ. By what means did the Christians conquer Rome? They conquered by love, sacrifice, and total giving, up to the cost of their very lives. History is witness that no empire can withstand the army of sacrificial love. And this history shall be repeated.

Humanity has not known clearly the definition of good and evil. We could not be certain where to commit ourselves, when to act, what to serve. This has been the source of the greatest confusion in human lives. We must not become the Christians who merely crave their own well-being. As Christians, we must live the life of Jesus and give ourselves totally for the benefit of others, so that others might have life. This is God's way.

This present world is evoking the wrath of God. It truly deserves His uncompromising judgment. But God is love, and He is long-suffering. God is suppressing His anger because He wants to save us. He is giving us a chance to change. He is waiting.

I know that Western culture is characterized by individualism. I tell you, *selfish* individualism is doomed. *Sacrificial* individualism will blossom. Individuality in itself is good. God gave each one of us a unique way to serve. But individualism without God can only build castles on the sands of decay.

I can see a great change, a great new surge of revolution coming to America—not by fire, not by bullets, but by God's truth kindling a revolution of the human heart. I have come here to ignite this spiritual revolution. The ultimate answer is not demonstrations or legal battles. The answer lies in the hearts of men and women, in the quiet revolution from selfishness to unselfishness.

Can you imagine how wonderful the ideal society will be? Individuals will belong to their families, the family will belong to the society, the society will belong to the nation, the nation will belong to the world, the world will belong to God, and God will belong to you. The person who gives the most will know God most deeply.

Some people might say to me, "Rev. Moon, you have some interesting theories, but their theological content must be examined more closely." But that is based upon a misunderstanding of me. I am speaking not from theory but from life. I am telling you that we are all here to live the truth, as Jesus lived the truth. This is not a theory, a philosophy, or a theological doctrine. It is the ultimate truth of God—not to be talked about, but to be lived.

When a people make this truth come alive, it is going to bring about a complete change upon the face of the earth. Although in one sense you know the truth of the things I have been saying, still nobody truly believes them. Since nobody believes the truth, nobody ever lives it. This truth is as old as God, yet as new as the 21st century. You must live the truth. If the revelation of the Unification Principle has made this age-old truth real in your heart, then you have in effect discovered a new truth. The Unification teaching is touching the hearts of millions of people, showing them the way to our very real God and Jesus Christ. People throughout the world are learning that God is absolute and perfect, and that the perfect God demands perfect human beings as His objects. Jesus said, "You, therefore, must be perfect, as your heavenly Father is perfect." (Matt. 5:48) He is clearly indicating that our standard of value is the perfection of our heavenly Father. Otherwise we cannot be God's objects and God cannot accept us.

All of us want to be perfect. All of us want heaven on earth, but we ask, "How can it be done?"

We wonder if it is at all possible for human beings to be perfect. Some contend, with apparent justification, that all one has to do is merely look at the human race to see the gross error of such an aspiration. We point to the sin and suffering inherent in all things, even in the things that are most holy. We say, "Only God is perfect." However, when we fully comprehend the design for men and women in God's concept of creation, we will understand that perfection is within our grasp.

In God's ideal of creation we were designed as temples of God, temples of the spirit of God, where God is master. "Do you not know that you are God's temple and that God's spirit dwells in you?" (I Cor. 3:16)

We were designed to be God's temples. When we attain this status, we shall cease to possess a will that is corruptible. Boundaries and laws will no longer be necessary, for His will is our will. With His spirit dwelling in us completely we shall move only as He guides us. We shall then be perfect because the force that is guiding and directing us is the perfect force.

When we achieve this ultimate goal we are in perfect union with God. We are no longer living on the human level alone, but on the divine level. We take on God's qualities because the Spirit dwells in and possesses us as a perfect temple; we reflect God's virtue and power. Thus we can be as perfect as the heavenly Father is perfect. This was the original pattern which God intended for humankind through Adam and Eve.

Marriage is the most important means of establishing God's kingdom on earth. Adam and Eve were God's first children. They were born of God, grew up in God, and were to have matured into perfection in God. God intended to make Adam and Eve one in heavenly matrimony. Then they would have borne sinless children and become the true mother and father for all humankind. They would have been the "True Parents," establishing the Heavenly Kingdom on earth.

Has such a kingdom ever existed? No. Instead, history started off in the wrong direction. From the first evil step, Satan has been the god of this world. It has, therefore, been God's purpose of restoration, His purpose of salvation, to restore the perfected family so that He can truly have His kingdom upon the earth. For this God needs a model. Who can set the criteria of perfection on this earth? To meet this need, the Messiah comes.

The history of God's providence is a sad, sad story. To comfort the heart of God and fulfill His work, we must clearly understand His process of restoration, and the poverty of the human response to God, especially at the time of Christ.

Jesus came to this earth to be the true, everlasting father of humankind. That's why he said true believers would deny their false parents, false society and false relationships—to come to their true father. The essence of Christianity is the tradition of true love. But while he was doing this important mission, Jesus was crucified. There was no chance for the tradition of true love to blossom fully in Jesus's time, and Jesus was not installed as everlasting father before his crucifixion.

When God created humankind, He placed Adam and Eve, man and woman, in the Garden of Eden. They both united with Satan and became sinful, thereby leaving God isolated. In the process of restoration, God must restore both Adam and Eve. Jesus came as the sinless Adam, or perfected Adam. He came as Messiah, as the model of perfection upon every level: The individual, family, tribal, national, and world-wide levels. He came to establish a perfect world in his lifetime, not over a period of centuries. This is why I Cor. 15:45 says Jesus is the "last Adam," the second Adam. His first mission was, therefore, to restore his bride and form the first family of God. All fallen generations would have been grafted onto him as the true olive tree. God-centered families, tribes, and nations would thus have been restored. Perfection would have reigned. The sinless state of God's kingdom could have been a reality for the last 2,000 years.

What sets Jesus apart from all other religious leaders? First, he said, he was the only begotten son of God, and therefore, that he possessed the entire love of God. When you have your first child, he or she is the center of a tremendous outflow of your love. If human beings feel such ecstatic joy with their first child, what about God? Because God sees His own image in his first son and through him can manifest His image to the entire world, you know how critical that person is. What should that son do? Does God need only a son? God knew ahead of time that He needed a pair, which would include a daughter. We have to talk about God's daughter, especially here in America! God will be more accepted in this country when we talk about His only begotten daughter as well.

A son living by himself would be like a person with one foot. Jesus knew that God was looking forward to having His only begotten daughter, so Jesus looked forward to restoring a woman in that position. This is why a central theme in the New Testament is that of bride and bridegroom. Christians today have to settle for a rather abstract view of this marriage relationship, saying that men as well as women are in the position of bride to Jesus, and not only that but that the church is as well. What has the church as an institution to do with Jesus' bride? Without question there is a certain symbolic meaning here, but God's ultimate desire is to give a physical bride to His son.

How could Jesus kiss an institution? Is it true that your President is such an institution that he doesn't know how to kiss? Are great leaders so great that they don't need to kiss anyone? Jesus was the King of Kings; in that sense he was the greatest institution so he should remain single the rest of his life, right? No, he was human and needed a wife like all other men. Would he sit on his throne and proclaim the single way of life as the most holy, dictating it to his subjects? Such a teaching would be a crippled teaching.

Suppose Jesus had been blessed with a perfect bride. Do you think that because he was a holy man, Jesus should have kept five feet away from her all the time? Would he have kissed his bride only for the sake of some sacrifice, or because he really wanted to show his love to her? As a holy man would he have looked at his bride just from time to time and then gone away, or would he have had fervent love in his heart to pour out upon his bride? Would he have been a sinner if he had done that?

Jesus came to fulfill the will of God, and to do so he had to restore his own bride. The entire Christian world is shaken at hearing this revelation, and because of it Christians have called me a heretic. Jesus can hear all this conversation going on here on earth. Do you think he would smile at hearing me say he should have had his own bride, or do you think he remained single because he thought that was the most holy way of life? Who created men and women, and who was Jesus' parent? God created men and women to become one, to marry and live as husband and wife. That is the holiest relationship of all in God's creation. Genesis says that God created Adam and Eve; God never said "It is good" until after he had created both Adam and Eve. Many religions have advocated a life of celibacy. The Unification Church is saying that families, not individuals, are the building blocks of the Kingdom of Heaven.

Jesus not only said that he was God's only begotten son, he also denied the world. No matter how beautiful or wonderful the world seemed, it was nothing in the sight of God, so Jesus' ministry had to begin with a denial of the world. Jesus came as the only begotten son to restore God's only daughter and make God's only begotten family, nation and world. Jesus truly occupied the position of central saint because he was the most direct manifestation of God.

What is God's central theme, the one which would completely melt even His heart? God doesn't need money or power. When Jesus came and pronounced himself as God's only begotten son, it moved God as no other sound did before. Many righteous people had come on earth in the 4,000 years before Jesus, but if God had asked Jesus, "Do you think you are greater than Moses and Abraham and all the others?" Jesus would have replied that he was. There has never been another person who could make exception to Jesus' claim, or even be a candidate for that position. In Jesus' mind, being God's son was such an absolute matter that nothing could shake it. Such a man or woman had never existed before.

Jesus reached the very center of love in the heart of God and he was always ready to receive any kind of instruction from God. No other saint has ever so closely embodied that goal. All the other saints taught a good way of life and truth, but no one was so absolute both in faith that God was their Father and in the total denial of the world as Jesus was. When he called himself the only begotten son of God, he meant that he and God were the only true existence and that he meant to change the rest of the world to become true as well. The first thing he intended to recreate was God's daughter. Then he intended to create God's family, society, nation and world.

The bell of such a refreshing sound had never rung before Jesus came. The sound of Jesus' bell resounded not only around the world but through the spiritual world. That sound pierced the very mind and heart of God and they resounded and rang together. That sound shook God and made Him feel good because it was the sound of love.

Why does He need love? Because God wants to be intoxicated in the joy of love. Only love can totally intoxicate Him in earth-shaking laughter and joy. That joy would not inspire only song and dance, but much more. God wants to be melted by love to the degree that He forgets Himself and His dignity as God and can become totally like a child.

Before God sent His champion Jesus Christ, He prepared the field with the chosen nation of Israel. This was the foundation for the Messiah's coming. The people of Israel could have perfected themselves and their nation if they had united with the coming of the Lord. The kingdom of God would have been a physical reality at that time.

Jesus' intention was directed only at building the Kingdom of God here on earth, but practically speaking, what is the Kingdom of God? The Bible doesn't say clearly, but the Kingdom of God Jesus was trying to build here on earth followed a simple teaching: As much as you love God your Father, that much you must love your country, your society and your own home. When that one tradition of love links every aspect of life, the Kingdom of God shall become a reality. When everyone worships one God as their common Father then no barriers will remain—no national boundaries or walls of language or denomination. Every barrier can be broken down.

If Jesus had just come to establish a new religion then he was not the Messiah. In reality Jesus couldn't care less about religion; what he cared about was a God-centered kingdom and that kingdom cannot be built by religion. That kingdom will be built by the family. Jesus came to build the first true family so that he could bring God down to a real home where He could dwell as the sovereign, as the true Father. There is no other way God's will could be fulfilled. There is no other way to build the Kingdom of God here on earth.

But Jesus was not accepted by his nation. Instead of welcome, he met rejection at every level. Jesus was denied the opportunity to take a bride in the position of restored Eve, and to establish the first God-centered heavenly family. Instead, he was nailed to the cross. Thus, the mission of Jesus Christ was left incomplete on earth. And this is why

Jesus promised his second coming. Jesus Christ must come again to consummate the mission of the Messiah. Let me repeat: Jesus was the perfected Adam and his mission was the restoration of humankind. The crucial step was to restore his bride, Eve. Jesus was a man, one with God, but he was not God the Father. When he returns to earth he will come as a man in the position of the third Adam.

These are revelations to me from God, and I want you to understand fully the main points. God intended Adam and Eve to come together in heavenly matrimony in the Garden of Eden. Since it was not realized at that time, God intended Jesus to fulfill this marriage in his time. But it was not realized by Jesus either, because no one had faith in him as Messiah on earth.

Jesus was the second Adam. It was God's will for him to be blessed in heavenly matrimony with the second Eve, his restored bride. God intended him to bring forth upon this earth his own sinless children. Then Jesus and his bride would have become the True Parents for humankind, and all humankind would have found life by grafting onto them. In Revelation, at the end of the Bible, it shows us clearly that the end of God's ideal is this perfect man and perfect woman; when they rejoice, embracing in holy matrimony, this is inexchangeable for the entire universe. Once God has achieved this high ideal as a standard, then there will be more such individuals and families coming into existence; this is what God has been working for. So this is the highest ideal of God and highest ideal of humanity. This is the deepest desire of God and also the deepest desire of humanity. Only around this one center can all people and God eternally be happy and one.

Jesus cautioned the people: "You are of your father the devil" (John 8:44), because at the beginning point of human history we were born Satan's children. By the restoration of True Parents we will be reborn as children of our heavenly Father, God. This will mean full salvation as His true children, not merely salvation as the adopted children of which St. Paul writes (Rom. 8:23).

God's will was denied fulfillment in Jesus' time. That is why he is coming again. In the book of Revelation, there is the prophecy of the marriage of the Lamb. This marriage banquet will in fact take place. True Parents for all human-kind will be realized in our time. God will bring forth His true family upon the face of the earth. All people will be made new through the True Parents. All people will be empowered to bring sinless children into the world. This will be done when Jesus Christ reappears. The Kingdom of Heaven on earth will then begin. This will be the day of hope, the day of the coming of the Lord at the second advent.

This is the day when God's original ideal will be realized for the first time. This is the day when the dwelling of God is with men and women. God will be full of joy. His own son as perfected third Adam will initiate an entirely new history upon the earth. On that day, we shall become living images of God. God will bring His kingdom to earth.

This ultimate realization of the ideal has been the hope of God as well as the hope of all humanity. I pledge to you from the bottom of my heart that the realization of all this is at hand, in the fullness of God's time.

3

God's Providence
In The Scriptures

We know that the world we live in today is not literally God's kingdom. We learn that human history started off on the wrong footing, on the evil side. This is why the Bible says that the god of this world is Satan. Due to the human fall, Satan is abiding in us, in place of God. Accordingly, we are the incarnation of Satan. And you are in the lineage of Satan, instead of God. This is against God's law of creation. This is why in the religious world there have been many martyrs. In primitive religions people were sometimes killed as offerings or sacrifices. That represented in a deviated way the impulse to shed the satanic blood. In God's eyes, we are not people of His creation. We are not truly human beings, we are just satanic beings in the position of His enemies. We are the children of Satan, who is God's enemy. That is the result of the human fall.

This is why Jesus said, "You are of your father, the Devil." (John 8:44) Against God's desire, our first human ancestors fell in an unchaste, premature love relationship with each other. In order for us to have perfect restoration, we must have true parents, and we must be made part of their lineage by going through a process of rebirth. In the Bible we read that when Nicodemus visited Jesus and heard him talk about rebirth, he asked, "How can we go back into our mother's womb?" Jesus reportedly said to him, "You are a leader of Israel and still you don't know what rebirth means?" In conclusion, he said, "If you are not born again, you cannot enter the Kingdom of God."

To be born again and to become part of a new lineage is resurrection. Being men and women of the fall and born of satanic lineage we are destined to be reborn; then alone can we enter the Kingdom of God. The course of restoration is the way of reversing the course of the fall. This means that you must restore the original lineage. In order to change our satanic lineage into God's, we must live an ascetic life, a life which presents difficulties and hardships. In order for us to be restored, we must go through this course.

In the course of the fall, Adam and Eve believed Satan more than God. That was the first stage. In the course of the restoration we must believe in God strongly, absolutely. The end result of the fall was our satanic lineage, under Satan. Our blood became stained. In order for Jesus to make the condition for us to deny satanic lineage, he finally had to shed his blood. We have had to receive his blood in order to belong to his lineage. In Holy Communion, the wine symbolizes godly lineage. By partaking of bread and wine, it signifies that one comes to be of His lineage. So, we are removed in that manner from the satanic lineage to divine lineage.

Fallen humanity has been burdened by a debt of blood, sweat and tears. If you ask God to tell you some of His experiences since the fall, there is nothing else He can tell except a story of sweat and tears and blood. He has no other history but that. Most Christians truly don't know what God is all about. They imagine Him sitting on a glorious throne enjoying life, but that is not true at all.

Someone has to liberate God and He cannot do it Himself. The agony of parents, or of husband and wife, cannot be solved by themselves alone. The agony of parents can only be solved by children; the agony of a husband can only be solved by his wife, and the agony of a wife by her husband. The only way to liberate God from His sorrow is by becoming a son or daughter of filial piety to take over His agony.

God wanted to forgive Adam and Eve, but He was not in the position to forgive them, because they were in no state to be forgiven. We must imagine this: suppose there was another person who did not fall—a brother of Adam, who, standing intact from the fall, would go to the Father and beg Him to forgive his brother and sister; what would have happened? If that man, without having fallen, would go to God and ask Him to forgive his brother for the fall, and if he would tell the Father that he would help by taking on any responsibility himself; he would be willing to be beaten or anything else for the sake of the fall of his brother and sister, God could have forgiven them. This was supposed to be the way of forgiveness, or salvation of the fallen people.

A person who has not fallen can be said to have nothing to do with Satan. If God has that kind of individual, He can develop His providence of salvation with that one in the center. This type of person is "Abel," or one who is in the position of Abel. Abel is supposed to be the person who can receive perfect love from God. He or she must be able to be triumphant over Satan. Abel must be able to sacrifice him or herself for humankind. In other words there should be one who is willing to be sacrificed in place of the fallen brother and sister in order to liberate them.

That sacrifical brother will become the Christ. What is the mission of Christ, the Messiah? He is the one who bears your burden and your indemnity. That is why he is the savior. If you take over the burden of someone else's life then you are that person's savior. Your fallen brother or sister will be liberated on that condition alone. With the coming of that person among humankind, there can be the hope of salvation. The gate of salvation will be opened with those tears which are to relieve God's sorrow and human sorrow.

Then why do we need the Messiah? What is his purpose? It is to bring us back to the point connecting to God's love. We want to go back to that point, but we have inherited satanic lineage. The blood lineage of fallen people is disconnected from God's love. This must be indemnified. Indemnity means ultimately that the original sin must be removed. How to remove original sin; that is the fundamental problem. Fallen people by themselves cannot do it. Therefore, the Messiah is necessary. Yet to send the Messiah, it was necessary for humanity to make some sort of conditional foundation acceptable to God.

In pursuing this goal, it has been the strategy of God to summon champions out of this evil world. To understand God's ways, let us examine the history of His providence.

The family of Adam was the first family in God's creation. In this family there was a man, Abel, whom God chose to be His first champion. Abel served God wholeheartedly, and became the first man to give up his life for God's purpose. Abel had to reject Satan and come back to the bosom of God by fighting against and defeating Satan. He had to separate himself from Satan and be different from his fallen brother. Since he was in that position he could receive God's love. These three stages are the important formula: the one who is willing to save the world must fight against Satan and win the victory over him; then he or she must come into the love of God; and then, feeling the heart of God and fallen people, he or she must be willing to sacrifice him or herself in place of the fallen people. Only on that condition can the fallen people be taken back.

Thus, Abel should have separated himself from Satan, or Cain, come into the love of God, and then, by feeling and experiencing God's grief and his brother's grief, should have sacrificed himself in place of them. Instead of being arrogant, Abel should have been willing to die for Cain. He should have saved his brother at the risk of his life, at the very price of his life.

Abel was not to be sacrificed by being killed; he was to have been a living sacrifice so that God could work through him. He was to sacrifice without being sacrificed by Satan; his sacrifice on the altar was offered to God. But in the process of doing that, he was killed by Cain.

Later on God called Noah as His champion. And Noah accomplished a very unusual mission. God directed Noah to build a ship, and he was to build it on the top of a mountain. Now, it is just common sense that in building a ship you need a shipyard by some body of water. But Noah's instructions were to build the ark on top of a mountain rather than at the seashore or riverside. How many of us here could accept that kind of mission? How many of us could obey such a command and set to work without a single shred of doubt?

In Noah's time, no one could believe that Noah had received a command from God—nor did anyone accept him in his mission revealing the coming flood judgement. Can you imagine how Noah appeared to the people of his day? For 120 years he went up and down, up and down that mountain working on his boat. Would anyone among the ladies in the audience like to think of herself in the position of the wife of Noah? I don't think you would be a very happy wife.

Noah's wife must have packed his lunch basket every day, using only a little food. Noah was so busy with the ark he could not find time to provide for his family. Within only a few months the family squabbles must have begun, but it was not just for twelve months or twelve years that Noah's wife had to sustain her situation, but for 120 years. Why, then, did God ask of Noah such an incomprehensible mission? Why does God have to work that way? There is a reason. It is because of evil.

God cannot dwell together with evil. The direction of God is 180 degrees contrary to the direction of evil. God abhors evil! God cannot accept the things that the evil world accepts. So God does not want anything to do with the evil world, or with whatever is tainted by evil.

We are all in the image of God and can find traits similar to His in our human nature. Consider if you have an enemy toward whom you have strong feelings; you don't want to so much as look at that person. Likewise, God will have nothing to do with the evil, Satanic world. Therefore, in dealing with it, He chooses ways often incomprehensible to human beings.

God also wants to test the faith of men and women. He cannot do this by asking just ordinary things of people. We must be willing to comply with God's extraordinary instructions. We must display to God absolute faith. This is not an easy task. People thought Noah was a crazy man for building the ark. Nobody knew he occupied the central position in God's view.

Not only Noah, but other people of God seem to act in peculiar ways when they are seen from the worldly viewpoint. Let us take a look at Abraham.

God summoned Abraham, not from a family headed by a man of God, but from an idol-maker's house, and ordered him to separate himself from his evil surroundings and leave his homeland. God wanted Abraham to be His champion. This was God's personal command. If Abraham had then discussed this matter with his father, the idol-maker would undoubtedly have asked him, "Are you crazy?" Abraham knew better than to mention anything to his father about his instructions from God. Who would have believed him? His mission was not just to say hello to his next door neighbor. God instructed him to journey to a strange land, as far away as Egypt.

Abraham's decision then was a lonely one, based upon his faith and his reliance upon God. By faith alone he made his decision and departed, with nothing on his mind except following the command of God. I know he stole away in the middle of the night. Suddenly he found himself wandering like a gypsy. He lived in self-denial; he had given up everything.

The champions of God have one characteristic in common: They begin their missions by denial of themselves and their surroundings. Isaac's son, Jacob, was no exception. Jacob was a man with strong will power in service to God. He wanted to serve God in an unprecedented fashion. He wanted to open an exemplary path, accomplishing something nobody else could duplicate.

In the Bible there are many stories about Jacob. One describes a very cunning act when he bought his elder brother's birthright in exchange for bread and a pottage of lentils. And later on he stole his father's blessing, which was intended for his elder brother Esau. In this incident Jacob knew beyond any doubt that he would make an enemy out of his elder brother. He committed himself nonetheless. That craving in Jacob, that ardent desire for God's blessing, was so strong in his heart that God was really comforted. After obtaining Isaac's blessing, Jacob then escaped the danger of being killed by his elder brother when he fled from his homeland and went to the strange land of Haran.

For 21 years Jacob endured a life of tribulation in Haran. During that time Jacob was repeatedly deceived by his uncle Laban. Ten times Laban cheated Jacob, and Jacob did not complain even once. He just persevered and waited for the day when he could return to his blessed homeland.

Then, in what manner did Jacob set up a tradition of belief enabling him to receive God's blessing and protection? It may appear simple, but Jacob and an offering alone were not enough; there was something else needed. The offering had not to be for the sake of Jacob himself; he had to offer it for the sake of the Israelites and their nation which was the nation of God's choice. In other words, the sacrifice is something to be offered in order to expand things to higher and wider dimension and more public nature, such as to the family and national dimension, and to have those things reach God and connect with Him. Whether or not you are strong in this idea can determine whether or not you receive God's blessing and cooperation.

The more opposition and persecution Jacob received from Laban, the more he thought of his native home where he had to bring back what he could get from Laban. He did not want merely to enjoy his life in Haran with the blessings God had allowed him to have, but he desired to share his blessing with his brother and parents back in his native home. This desire to share with his own family was the basis or beginning of his idea to love his own people and then the nation.

Jacob's primary desire was to share all the blessings he had with his brother and parents and thus to become harmonized in oneness with them. Jacob led the lonely life of a shepherd, but all during this time his ultimate purpose was not to gain money or the material blessing. He missed his native home. He felt sorry for what he had done to his elder brother. He thought it was understandable for Esau to want to kill him when he had taken away the birthright by cheating; and he was sympathetic with his brother.

What Jacob had that was acceptable as an offering to God was that the more difficult and lonely his situation became, due to the aggravating persecution from Laban, the deeper attachment he felt towards his parents and brothers. This made him always wonder what he could do for their sake; this was his primary question. He thought that he could readily share with everybody at home what he had acquired by spending twenty one long years of drudgery. If he felt the least bit self-centered, thinking that all the things he acquired belonged to himself alone, Jacob would have ended his course in failure. This was the case because God blessed Jacob not for his own welfare and prosperity, but so that he could lay the foundation on which all the Israelites could enjoy the blessing. In other words, Jacob had to think in terms of public benefit in order to succeed. When Jacob completed his twenty one year course successfully, God blessed him with material wealth and all the other things necessary for his mission.

That day finally came, and at the ford of Jabbok, on the way back home, God sent an angel to fight with Jacob. Now consider this: An angel from God suddenly appeared to Jacob and became a dreadful enemy. God was really pressing Jacob and testing the strength of his faith. Jacob had to wrestle with the angel. And he did wrestle.

Jacob didn't cease fighting all through the night. He never gave up. And then God knew that Jacob's determination was to fight to the end, even to death. What was the motivation and significance of the wrestling? If Jacob should be defeated by the archangel, all his possessions, all his children, himself and his wives, which should have been unified into wholesome oneness, could have been torn into pieces by satanic hands. However, if he should win, all those things would belong to him and God.

They fought all through the night until they were both exhausted, but the wrestling match was not over yet. How do you think the match went? They were not evenly matched. There were times when Jacob was almost defeated. What do you think? Was it Jacob who fell more times or the archangel? It is understandable that Jacob fell more times, but he did not give up even though he faced death; he fought desperately to win over the archangel. He would cling to the archangel again and again at the risk of his life. That's what made him fierce. That's exactly what happens in our course of life in faith. You are desperate to win over Satan, but Satan is so fierce that you stumble over and over again. No matter how many times you may be on the verge of defeat, you will attack him again and again.

The archangel knew that he had to leave Jacob at daybreak. So, just before dawn, he became desperate and broke Jacob's thigh. How do you think the archangel broke Jacob's thigh? He must have done this in a moment when Jacob was weak. If, at that moment, Jacob was not being defeated, he could not have done that. Still, Jacob could not give up. Even though his thigh was broken, Jacob could not give up. At the thought of loss he became even more furious, and attacked the angel again and again. He would rather lose his life in attacking than lose the battle. Jacob finally won the test. The angel of God surrendered, and said to him, "Your name shall no more be called Jacob, but Israel, for you have striven with God and with men, and have prevailed." (Gen. 32:28)

Now Jacob was on his way home to meet his brother Esau. He could have gone somewhere else to enjoy his wealth if he did not think of God's will. He could have said, "Esau is Esau, and I am I; what have I to do with his life?" But his mind was so occupied with God's will that he wanted to meet his brother and reconcile the past and soothe his heart until his resentment vanished. What did he have to do in meeting his elder brother, Esau? First of all, he was ready to give up all his possessions, all his servants and his children, telling his brother that all these belonged to him. His attitude was: "All that I have is yours except God's will and God's blessing which is eternally mine." Adam, who ignored God's will, was self-centered, minding only himself, and lost his children and all things of God's blessing. On the contrary, Jacob was so God-centered that he would give away all things for the will of God. This is what made Jacob different from Esau. Thus, on the family level, Jacob could wrestle with Esau and risk all that he had in his possession. Jacob would think to himself, "Esau, you cannot have all this wealth if you don't excel me in exalting God's will." He would challenge and deal with his brother with this attitude. He thought, "As long as you take these possessions of mine, it means that you are one with me and exalting God's will."

After receiving Jacob's gifts, Esau's heart melted. Thus the two brothers who had hitherto felt resentment and hostility toward one another embraced, shedding tears and blessing each other. A new era of history opened at this time on a higher dimension. There, Esau also shared in the blessing of being Israel, the victor. Jacob's course may look simple, but there is a historical meaning in it since all the things which had to be carried out under the providence of God were condensed in his course.

Later on God chose Moses as His champion. Imagine how fortunate Moses was to grow up in the Pharaoh's palace, where he could enjoy a luxurious life. But then one day as a young man he suddenly stood up as the champion of his people; he could no longer stand the Egyptians' oppression of his people. At that moment he knew that God was with him. He rejected his surroundings, denied himself, and went to the wilderness of Midian. He awaited his ultimate mission for forty years, persevering and growing worthy of God's blessing. Moses's life was very humble and meek. Every day he surrendered himself anew to God's purpose and asked His divine guidance, cagerly awaiting his eventual mission, the leading of his people out of Egypt.

These men, Abel, Noah, Abraham, Jacob, and Moses, were champions of God. Now let us look also at John the Baptist. Described in the Bible as a great saint and prophet, John the Baptist went around the countryside like a common vagabond. He went without shoes, wearing camel skin with a leather belt, sustaining himself on locusts and wild honey. This was not a customary way to live, even in John's time; and I don't think John the Baptist's parents were very proud of their son. They must have felt ashamed.

Suppose you put yourself in the position of parents with your son, John The Baptist, going out in the wilderness year after year and living like a beggar. How would you feel? I have traveled in Israel, and I don't believe you will find many locusts or much wild honey in the desert. John the Baptist had to beg for his food many times. Imagine him wearing a camel skin, half of his body exposed, barefoot and with a beard, going from one place to another begging for food. If I came up here on the podium tonight barefoot, with a beard and clothed in an animal skin, and then said I was proclaiming the word of God, I am sure you would think I was crazy.

We must be curious about the objectives and motives of these providential figures. All of these great men started their life of faith centered not on themselves, but on God. Why do we have to respect and honor them, and give them credit for their contribution? Simply because they received instruction from God, not from themselves. Also, we should know what kind of life they lived for God in that age. We find that they had a conflict—their life of faith versus the life of reality. We find that they were not of one will when they faced a conflict. Also, we find that they solved the problem when they centered on God, and not on themselves. Also, we know that because of this conflict between God's side and the world's side, they multiplied their persecution and suffering. That is why they are great people!

Always we find that their life in this world was lonely because they suffered many, many things and were persecuted by this world. When they had nobody to convey their thoughts and feelings to, they could go only to God and talk to Him. Also, when we look at their lives in the world, their material lives—they were so narrowed down, received so few material things; naturally, they turned their hearts and lives toward God. When we think of how they were living in this world, their scope of consciousness was so narrowed down that they had to cognize everything centered on God. That was their life.

Naturally they had to live their lives centering on oneness with God. In every area—recreation with others, knowledge and cognition—they plunged themselves into a relationship with God, because there was no one else to rely on except God. There was no place to have give and take horizontally, to seek the object, so they concentrated on finding their object in God, more seriously than they sought an object in this world. Because the reality of this world for them was so narrow, they had to rely on heaven to get through such a narrow opening to God—and thereby they opened a new realm by embracing God.

Even if a narrow detour must be taken to God, they, and we, are not supposed to be depressed. There is a way out. We cannot be discontented. God created all things for the purpose of happiness and satisfaction and contentment. When we reach this narrow detour, we are going to find a way out with the help of God. that is the place where true happiness and contentment will be. From that narrowed-down point, the new relationship between God and ourselves will begin to open. For example, St. Francis emphasized pure poverty, a nothingness in which he could find happiness, appreciation, contentment, and satisfaction. From that point on, God could move and let him feel happiness and joy. Oneness with God can be created from that point. We have to realize that we as fallen people are standing in the center of two lines, between the world's side and God's side. We have to know when to narrow down, so we will know when the new era of happiness and joy will begin.

Let us continue along this line and examine the situation of Jesus Christ himself. I am sure there are many devout Christians among you who have various opinions on the life of Jesus. How would you visualize Jesus's appearance? What was Jesus doing for the thirty years before his public ministry? Was he in a college studying? The Bible doesn't say he even went to elementary school. He was a laborer, an assistant to a carpenter. There is so much to know, so many hidden truths within the Bible which are not written explicitly. If I revealed some of those secrets I am sure you would be amazed. Even though I know these things, I could not tell you those stories lightly. For you then would ask, "How do you know such things?"

I learned them from Jesus. Yes, and I learned from God. Remember, at the time of Noah nobody could believe Noah. At the time of Abraham, nobody could believe Abraham. By the same token, even though I will honestly tell you what actually happened at the time of Jesus, no one will easily believe me.

Who is the Messiah? The Messiah is completely united with the heart of God, like a direct import to earth from heaven. When God sent Jesus to be the Messiah, did He just take him as a baby and place Him on earth, or did He at least have to utilize the body of a woman for him to be born?

Jesus was born of Mary, so does this mean Mary was God? Did Mary have her own parents here on earth or did she drop out of the sky? Since Mary had parents, she must have been a descendant of the fallen lineage. Even though

Mary also came from fallen parents there must be proof that she had nothing to do with the fallen lineage. Further, we must ask the question, how do we know Jesus Christ is truly the Son of God? What is the proof? As far as the actual work of religion is concerned, Buddha did a far greater job, as he had many more disciples in his own lifetime. The same is true of Confucius. Mohammed also was a much more successful religious leader than Jesus. What is the criteria for us to say that Jesus is the Son of God?

The explanation begins with the same principle: Jesus is the Son of God because he came out of the heavenly lineage, whereas the other religious founders, like Buddha, Confucius and Mohammed, did not come from that heavenly lineage. No matter how much they accomplished, they didn't have the same qualification as Jesus Christ.

To understand how Mary was separated from the fallen lineage, we must refer back to Jacob and his immediate descendants. Jacob and Esau were about the age of forty when they finally fulfilled the will of God; however, their success could only affect those people of that age or older. No one below the age of forty could benefit by this progress in the restoraton. Therefore, God prepared another step in His dispensation that would protect His children from the period of their life in their mother's womb until the age of forty. This providence was sealed within the next three generations of Jacob's descendants. It is recorded in Genesis chapter 38.

Judah was the fourth son of Jacob, and Judah's first son married a woman whose name was Tamar. According to the Law, if a son died without leaving sons, his brother must act as a husband to the dead brother's wife so that the dead brother's lineage would be continued. Tamar did not have children when her husband died, and when the next brother refused to fulfill his responsibility, he also died. Tamar saw that through the third brother as well, she had no hope to bear children.

She knew that her mission was to continue the family of her husband and Judah, his father, and she finally decided to sacrifice even her honor in order to fulfill. Disguising herself as a prostitute, Tamar enticed her father-in-law to have a relationship with her. Without knowing she was his daughter-in-law Judah consented. At that time adultery was punished by death. In order to save her life for the sake of her child, Tamar asked Judah for his signet and staff as a pledge for payment, and then confiscated them.

Three months later when it became obvious that the widow Tamar was pregnant, she was brought before Judah to be judged. You can imagine Judah's horror, "Bring her out, and let her be burned!" But she answered, "By the man to who these belong, I am with child," and she brought out the things that Judah had given her in his pledge.

Adam and Eve fell through fornication, and Tamar was one example of how God frequently used women of most unusual character in restoration. Why would God use adulterous women in the dispensation? They are acting in a satanic position, but if insodoing they deny satanic nature by complete obedience to God, then they can be restored from one extreme to the opposite extreme.

God selected His champions from the most miserable situations. Tamar was a righteous woman, and though she was placed in a sinful position, she completely dedicated herself to God's mission, risking her life, honor, and prestige. Paralleling the way Eve lied to God and her husband-to-be in the process of the fall, Tamar deceived her father-in-law and her husband-to-be, Judah's third son. She reversed the position of Eve by reversing Eve's actions, and the significant thing is that she risked her life in doing it, just as Eve did in falling at the cost of her life. Thus, God could have a claim on Tamar's womb—on the very life emerging in that womb.

Tamar conceived twins, and the struggle of Cain and Abel began within her very womb. The Bible records how Rebecca's twins also struggled within their mother's womb. Rebecca prayed to God to understand what was happening, and the Lord answered her, saying, "Two nations are in your womb, and two peoples, born to you, shall be divided;

the one shall be stronger than the other, and the elder shall serve the younger." Ultimately Jacob did gain the birthright from his elder brother, Esau.

When the time came for Tamar's children to be delivered, the struggle ensued directly within her womb. The first child started to come out and the midwife tied a red thread around his wrist. That sign foreshadowed the emergence of communism in the last days. Esau was also named "Edom," which means "red." (Gen. 25:30) However, before the first child could be born there was a struggle, and the younger brother pulled the other back inside the womb and was himself born first. That son was named Perez, and the other named Zerah. The result of this struggle is that for the first time the restoration of Cain and Abel took place inside the mother's womb, the younger brother having subjugated his elder brother even prior to birth. Tamar's extraordinary action cleansed Judah's lineage and rendered it intact from satanic invasion from the time of conception.

Through this victory at the time of Tamar and also Jacob's earlier victory, God could claim a foundation that spanned the entire human lifespan. Jesus was born in the lineage of Judah, and Satan had no way to invade his life in the womb because the cleansing process was already completed. Jesus came years after the dispensation of Jacob and Tamar because God had to wait for Israel's national foundation to be established. The conditions were fulfilled on the family level at the time of Jacob, Tamar and Judah, but God needed to create a foundation to receive the Messiah within a nation, that he might be received on the national and international levels as easily as possible.

Finally, God chose a woman whose name was Mary. Mary was a revolutionary woman of faith who could follow God's revolutionary tactics. Because the fall came through the archangel, an angel was needed to assist Mary by bringing her God's revelation. Mary completely believed what the angel told her of her mission; the angel told her that she would conceive, and the child would be great and holy, and that his name should be called Jesus.

Mary's situation paralleled Eve's in the garden of Eden. Mary and Joseph were engaged but not yet married; Adam and Eve were also in an engagement period as they were maturing. An angel brought Eve to the fallen act, but an angel brought Mary to the fulfillment of the heavenly dispensation. Mary was also in a position to deceive her husband and father. Do you think Mary could discuss with her father or Joseph about the miraculous conception of her baby? She was risking her life because in those times an adulterous woman was to be stoned to death.

Mary was the third providential woman to be picked by God. Through the previous victories of Rebecca and Tamar all satanic conditions had been cleared from Jesus' lineage, and even though Mary conceived Jesus outside of marriage, Satan could not accuse her. Even inside his mother's womb Jesus was already the only begotten Son of God, and after his birth everything he did was with the authority of the Son of God.

Without having an entirely different beginning, there was no way that Jesus could be the Messiah, the begotten Son of God. What's the difference between Jesus and any other child with physical parents? The difference is historical time; on the surface the parents may look the same but their backgrounds are entirely different. Mary was a historic figure. Throughout thousands of years of history God and Satan bargained and struggled and finally reached an agreement even before Mary herself came into being. God knew that He had to use a woman's body to have His son born on this earth, and in order to have that one woman ready God prepared for thousands of years.

Nonetheless, from the point of view of the society of those days, Jesus was a fatherless child, an illegitimate child. In the sight of God he was conceived by the Holy Spirit, but there was no way to prove it to people! So set your thoughts in a realistic vein and just evaluate what I am going to say.

Mary conceived Jesus before marriage. Under the Jewish law, such a woman was to be condemned to death by stoning. Joseph suffered indignation because of Mary's situation, and quietly waited until the right time to end their engagement. Then an angel appeared to Joseph and said to him, "You are to take Mary as your wife. Do not condemn her, for she has a special mission from God." If Joseph had not been a righteous man, Mary would have been automatically condemned to death by stoning.

Now, do you think Joseph could have discussed this matter with his parents by saying, "Mother and father, my wife-to-be, my betrothed, has conceived a child, but an angel said that this is the will of God, so I must take her as my wife and care for her"? What would Joseph's parents have said? There are many older couples in the audience tonight. Put yourself in the position of the parents of Joseph. You would not have believed Joseph if he spoke such things. Again, Joseph had to make a lonely decision. Without discussing the matter with anybody, he took his fiancee off to some secret hiding place.

Now consider them going towards Bethlehem. It was almost the time for Mary to give birth. If the environment was such that she could have prepared things for the coming child, she would have done that, but she could not prepare anything for the child. When the child was born, she laid him in a stable manger and wrapped him in swaddling clothes. If Jesus had had physical relatives united with Mary and Joseph, would they not have helped Mary prepare the way beforehand? From all those things we can gather that Mary gave birth to the child in a lonely, lonely situation.

At the time of Jesus' birth, God sent three wise men. They were led to that place by God and should have ministered to Jesus, raising him until the day of his marriage. What would have happened if the wise men, when told to go back to their country through different ways than they expected to go, had taken mother Mary and the holy child with them back to their country? If Jesus had been raised there in concealment, the wise men would have become world-famous historical figures.

I don't know if they were from one nationality or from

three different nationalities; it would have been even better if they were from three different nationalities. If, after Jesus was brought to one of the three nations, he was still being persecuted, they could remove him to other nations. If they had helped Jesus to grow up wholesomely, completely safe from satanic invasion, how famous they would have become! Then the wise men could have been Jesus' disciples. Things would have been much better. Since nothing like that took place, Jesus had to look for his own disciples, as you know.

I am sure Joseph went through a most difficult period in which he was full of suspicion about Mary. Joseph must have asked his wife-to-be, "Mary, we are close and have no secrets from one another. Now tell me what really happened to you. Who is the true father of the baby in your womb?" I am sure any husband would be very curious about this matter. If I had been in the position of Joseph I would have asked Mary this question. But Mary was telling the truth when she said, "I really do not know who is the father of this child. It was conceived by God." How many of us could believe her statement? It is easier to believe now, because we know who Jesus is, but this was not the case during the lifetime of Jesus.

Therefore, Joseph had certain suspicions and injured feelings in his heart. He thought, "My wife is not truly honest with me." Because of these circumstances there was emotional turmoil and upheaval in Jesus' family after he was born.

One incident in particular witnesses to this fact. One day Jesus met his mother at a wedding feast in Galilee, and Mary informed Jesus that they had run out of wine. He called out to his mother, saying, "O Woman, what have you to do with me? . . ." (John 2:4) The point is, he did not say, "Mother," but instead called out, "Woman." Later on a disciple of Jesus came to him saying, "Your mother and your brothers would like to see you." And Jesus replied, "Who are my mother and my brothers? . . . Here are my mother and my brothers! Whoever does the will of God is my brother, and sister, and mother." (Mark 3:33-35) This indicated that in the eyes of Jesus the members of his family were not doing the will of God.

Jesus suffered great anguish within his own family. There are many hidden stories not yet revealed. Many of the facts about his suffering are unknown. The Bible leaves a scanty record of the thirty years before Jesus' public ministry. If this were a glorious record, we can be sure that God and Jesus' disciples would have revealed it. But Jesus lived in sorrow and grief; he was an obscure figure for thirty years.

As a child, Jesus definitely knew that he was special. He heard what the common people thought about him but his own self-image was completely different. From the time he was small he could never talk openly in his own way. The only consolation he could seek was in communication with God, and he spent most of his time praying to God and seeking His guidance. As a result Jesus became stronger and stronger in this period and circumstances compelled him in only one direction—toward God and the realization of His ideal. He knew that humanity's thinking was vastly different from God's and that it had to be corrected; he also knew that society understood nothing about what God wanted and that he himself would have to change it. Because of his adverse circumstances Jesus had to really pray hard to God, to the point where God could talk to him and teach him what he would need for his future work. As Jesus grew older and knew more and more clearly who God was and what his own mission was supposed to be, his heart became heavier and more agonized and his environment became more difficult to tolerate.

Jesus' birthday—Christmas—meant nothing special in those days. The most precious friend for Jesus would have been the person who came to him, not with many presents or words of congratulations, but rather with a tearful heart to console him in his situation and to discuss with him what he was going to do in the future. If someone like this had been there then Jesus would have been far happier than if someone had come with presents. That person could have been one of his own brothers or sisters. Knowing his hidden suffering, he or she could have brought just a small piece of cake wrapped in a handkerchief to give to Jesus on his birthday, saying, "The people don't understand you, but I will try to help you. You must not be disappointed." Jesus certainly would have welcomed such a person far more than someone who came with a fancy present for him and then went away. If there had been one such brother or sister in Jesus' family then Jesus would have remembered him or her for a long time and would have spoken about it.

Jesus always wished that his own parents, brothers, and relatives could help him in the mission. If his parents would not help him, then who else would help? Jesus was the central figure, the personage of divine mission whom God sent after a preparation of 4,000 years. There were people prepared to receive him. In order for him to be able to establish the Kingdom of God on earth he must have been able to establish the Kingdom right in his own family first. He knew the heavenly law of the divine family, so his own family had to be placed under that law. According to that divine law, Joseph should have loved and ministered to Jesus, not to speak of his mother Mary. Jesus had even to educate his own parents and brothers and sisters; they had to love him more than anyone else, ministering to him and helping him in his mission. Jesus was a prince of the Kingdom of Heaven. He was not an ordinary prince of a kingdom on earth. He was the only son of God, and he was sent to do this mission as the single central figure sent by God. That family had to exemplify and build the tradition by ministering to the child, even though he was their son. In preparing food for him, in preparing clothes for him, in doing anything for him, they were to be very sincere and whole-hearted. Their other sons and daughters should have helped Jesus carrying out his mission. But the situation was in conflict—it was not like this. With all of these things happening in his environment, he had to lead an unhappy life preparing for his mission alone until the moment he was thirty years of age.

Jesus knew God's plan for himself, for Israel and for all the rest of humankind. God is immaterial, but by having a body Jesus could experience the existing human condition, and he knew that he had to be the central point to bring that world back to God. Do you think that he wanted very much for someone to show some understanding, or that he wanted to hear even one word of love spoken to him, knowing that without him no one had any chance to return to God? Jesus yearned to hear the high priest say, "We must prepare ourselves to receive you, because that's the only way for us to return to God."

Do we know of anyone who understood and said this? The leading people not only did not come near him, they even opposed him directly. People were therefore shocked one day when they heard him say, "I am the fulfillment of the Law." and "Moses wrote of me." He proclaimed, "I am the Son of God," and "The Father in heaven has sent me." "I am the Way, the Truth, and the Life; no one comes to the Father but by me." How many of us could have accepted such extraordinary statements if we had lived in those days? Jesus just bewildered people, he sounded so outrageous. Even John the Baptist had difficulty seeing Jesus as the Son of God, and John was supposed to prepare the people and make straight the way of the Lord.

Bringing the Kingdom of God here on earth on a nation-wide and then worldwide scale was Jesus' only goal. With this in his heart, what would Jesus have preached? Would he have said, "Brethren, I am the Son of God and I have many gifts and blessings for you. If you unite with me, I'll give you good homes, good lives and abundant blessings. I will even make you powerful kings and queens in the world." Wouldn't he have said instead, "Brethren, even if you and I must be sacrificed, God wants to save the world. Let us become champions for the salvation of the world."

Today it is very easy to accept Jesus Christ as the Son of God because for 2,000 years Christianity has been glorifying him as God. But in those days, the elders did not accept him. And the priests did not accept him either. They were no less intelligent than we are today. In fact, we would probably have compounded their mistakes if we had lived in the days of Jesus of Nazareth. They saw only an outcast, a blasphemer, and an outrageous heretic. They simply could not see the Son of God.

Jesus had been long-awaited. The Messiah was expected for 2,000 years. But when he finally appeared, there was no reception for him. The faith of the people of Israel at that time was no less powerful, no less devout than the faith of Christians today. Yet we know that the people Jesus associated with were not on a par with the rest of society, that he mixed with harlots, tax-collectors, and fishermen. We know the story that one day a young woman poured precious ointment over Jesus' body, then washed his feet with her hair. If we had seen these things, how many of us can say in a pious manner that we would have accepted Jesus as the Son of God?

Jesus made statements which rendered it almost certain he would be crucified. He said that anyone who loved his family more than Jesus was not worthy of Jesus, and that meant denying everyone. So everyone opposed him for encouraging division of families. People said Jesus was destroying the family bond and social ties.

The three years of Jesus' public ministry were a far cry from the anticipated Messiahship. No one understood Christ's true mission. People judged the Son of God with sinful eyes, according to their own earthly standards. And they treated him as they pleased. In the city of Jerusalem, Jesus was sometimes angered at the immoral behavior of the people. He even overturned the moneychangers' tables in a moment of force. By normal standards he should have been arrested and no civil court would have vindicated him. But under the law of God Jesus had not committed any sin. Civil law is not heavenly law. But this sinful world can never be hospitable to the purity of Christ.

As I mentioned, all the saints and prophets and righteous ones of history had first to deny themselves totally and give themselves up to God. When He summoned them, they gave up their homes, their fortunes, their families and their nations. God wants His champion on the individual level, on the family level, tribal level, national level and world-wide level. He has summoned His champions on each level. And the qualification for God's champion on any level always remains the same. He or she needs the absolute and untiring faith required to follow His command wherever it may lead. God needs total obedience to His will.

We must examine then, what is the will of God? Why does He give His people such a hard time? Salvation of the individual is certainly important in the sight of God. God does not neglect that. However, that is not the ultimate purpose of God's work. God's will is the salvation of the world! God needs an individual to be His champion for the ultimate goal of world salvation. God summoned one family to be an instrument for the salvation of the world. God summoned His people to achieve the salvation of the world. God wants to have a nation as His champion, for the ultimate fulfillment of world salvation.

People in the time of Jesus were anxiously awaiting the Messiah. But many were thinking only of their own national glory. They did not understand the universal mission of Jesus Christ. It was the purpose of God to send the Messiah to the chosen people of Israel so that the Messiah would unite with the chosen people. Then they could become soldiers of faith, to fight for and achieve the salvation of the world.

The foundation for the Messiah was laid through Jacob, the champion of the family, and through Moses, the champion of his people. Finally the Messiah came to the nation of Israel. He was to be the champion of the nation and the champion of the entire world. The purpose of God is not the salvation of one church or one nation alone. It is the will of God that He sacrifice the lesser for the greater. Therefore He will sacrifice the church or the nation for the world. If Christians today think only of their own salvation, their own heaven and their own well-being, then they are not living in accordance with the purpose of God. If we are only concerned with the salvation of our own families, we are not worthy of God's blessing. If people focus on benefiting their own people alone, or their nation alone, then they are absolutely going against the will of God.

God will give you your own salvation. When you become God's champion for world salvation, your own salvation is assured. Now, the Christian population is probably one-seventh of the total world population. But among these, very few are devout Christians. And among devout Christians, how many of us really strive for the salvation of humankind? We must all devote ourselves to the salvation of the world!

God cannot be pleased with us if we live in a self-centered way. I met Jesus personally, and I received a revelation through which I learned that God's grief is great. His heart is broken. Today God is working ceaselessly for the ultimate salvation of all humankind. He needs His champion to succeed in this work. The purpose of God's church is to save the entire world. The church—God's Israel—is the instrument of God, and it was this very fact that was forgotten at the time of Jesus.

During the Old Testament era people used the things of creation to make offerings. The physical offering was supposed to be made on the national basis with the symbol of the universal sacrifice for humanity being the Messiah. Why is the Messiah needed as the physical consummation of the sacrifice? Jesus Christ as the Messiah came as the sacrifice upon the altar of the nation of Israel, but the Messiah needed human beings to complete the sacrifice because they were to be benefited, not the Messiah. The Messiah does not come for himself but for humanity. The universal Messiah came to the nation of Israel, the universal altar, and the people were supposed to unite with him completely and thus be offered together on that altar. However, that unity was not there. Jesus was offered as the sacrifice on the altar, but there was no one to offer that sacrifice to God. There was no one united with Jesus.

What was the difference between Jesus and the lambs

which were offered in the Old Testament Age? The lambs were ignorant, but Jesus was fully aware of the wrong humankind had done and what was necessary to liquidate that sin, and at the same time he felt acute pain as the offering. Before Jesus, neither the offering understood nor did human beings fully understand why an offering was needed and what was wrong with human ancestry, but in Jesus' time the offering itself knew the totality of human sin.

How did Jesus make himself into an offering? By showing in his own life the path all humankind must go. In fact, Jesus very much wanted to say, "What I am doing now is what you should be doing instead, but since you don't understand I must show it to you." What way did Jesus go? Was it his way of life to fight with other people or display his power? Jesus didn't teach the people through knowledge; his teaching was much deeper than that. Certainly he was not exhibiting wealth to people. Simply said, he was showing the way to heaven. What was the way that Jesus went? The only crucial thing is to sacrifice oneself and establish true love.

Then why have suffering and sacrifice become necessary? It is for the same reason that someone in this world suffers after doing something wrong. We have so grossly violated God's law of the ideal that the ideal became impossible, and to offset this wrongdoing we are required to suffer. The Kingdom of Heaven and the love within man and woman had been lost and Jesus showed that it could not be recovered without paying a price; what he showed us was how to sacrifice. Why was it necessary for him and for everyone to sacrifice? At the price of his own suffering Jesus wanted to show us how to overcome sin.

Do you think sinners rejoiced because they had finally met the man who could free them from sin? Jesus brought with him all the love that was lost, but which response is more likely when the Messiah comes—that people will be happy and forget what they have done, or that they have to overcome a great turmoil of feeling before they can feel worthy of going to their savior? Can a person ignore what he or she has done wrong and come to the savior, or should he or she feel so much remorse over the gravity of sin in the past that he doesn't even know how to properly conduct himself? It is more likely that when one realizes the magnitude of one's sin one would tremble at the mere thought of the awesome difference between oneself and the Messiah.

When the Messiah comes to liquidate sin, is the sinner going to tell the Messiah what to do? Instead of telling Jesus what he should do, our feeling should be that we cannot even speak at all. Upon seeing him, the first thing you must experience is the shedding of so many tears that you cannot even see around you. After the fall humankind found such darkness around that we didn't know what to do, and these tears should produce such a drenching that you cannot see or do anything. Yet at the same time we should feel hope within us.

In the Old Testament times people made offerings without knowing their significance, but Jesus made his sacrifice for humankind in the awareness that he was dying for them. If a man or woman is willing to die for the Messiah then actual death may not be necessary. This has been a traditional value in Christianity, but we can see that compared to this standard modern Christianity has deviated from Jesus' teaching. We can live again by being completely willing to submit ourselves and die without making any demand. If a person is willing to die then that person lives and can dwell in heaven. This is what Jesus taught. When we gain our personal lives, however, that's only the beginning; then we have to die for the rest of humanity. And, we must make such a relationship with them that they are willing to die for us, and on that foundation we can go to heaven.

What would have happened if all twelve disciples had volunteered to be crucified before Jesus? What would the history of the world have been like? Do you think God would have resurrected only Jesus and not his disciples? No, God is impartial and loves everyone and certainly He would have resurrected them all. Would the disciples have ascended to heaven along with Jesus? They would not have forsaken the world but would have returned along with Jesus, and helped to revive all people on earth. Before the fall the angels were continually involved with the human world on earth, and the same ability would have been possible for the disciples.

Why did Jesus ascend to heaven by himself? It happened because there was no one who was willing to die with him. If everyone had been willing to die with Jesus, would God have raised the whole nation to heaven with Jesus? He might have, but since His purpose is to save the world God probably would have decided to create heaven on earth right then. The influence of Israel would have spread throughout the world in just a short period of time. If that had happened then human history would have culminated at that time and Christianity would never have gone through a history of bloodshed. God would have started the Kingdom of Heaven at that point and Jesus would never have had to come again.

Because Jesus went to heaven alone, it became necessary for the disciples also to shed blood and die before they could go to heaven. Only after that could they have deep relationship with Jesus. For 400 years Christians literally had to shed blood. Many people have wondered why God should require bloodshed and martyrdom of religious people, and now it is clear that all humankind had to go the way Jesus went.

When Jesus Christ was crucified on the cross, none who accepted him were there. The priests and all the disciples had disappeared. No one was there to offer Jesus as the sacrifice on the altar. An offering and sacrifice is presented to God for the sake of human beings, but if there is no one there to be benefited then how can the offering be given value? The only possible way that the sacrifice could still be effective was to consider that Jesus' spirit and body were separated.

In that way Jesus' body represented the nation, whereas

Jesus' spirit took the position of the actual sacrifice. By having his spirit one with God, Jesus made his sacrifice acceptable in the sight of God. Jesus' offering was accepted as a spiritual offering; the sacrifice he offered was a spiritual one. From that time, Jesus has been working on that base to establish the spiritual foundation, from the family to the society, nation, and world, until the time when the physical offering can be made.

Because the nation as a whole couldn't unite with Jesus, it was not restored and established as God's nation. To atone for this was Jesus' responsibility, so Jesus made a great sacrifice to preserve and expand God's sovereignty. With Jesus, the Old Testament Age of going to God through sacrifices ended, and a new age where Jesus himself became the sacrifice started. Christians long to become one with Jesus and God, which means that God, Jesus and human beings are united. That is the purpose of Christianity.

From this principle, Christianity emphasizes being one with Jesus Christ, saying: "Love Jesus Christ more than anybody else. By doing so, you can find salvation most directly, because Jesus already set the condition for spiritual salvation. Therefore, by uniting with him, you can quickly reach the goal." Christianity emphasizes how you can become one in heart with Jesus Christ. That is the central faith and belief. Your life should be completely parallel with that of Jesus; that is the secret, to share even the sorrow of Jesus Christ. When he is joyful, you can be joyful; when he is working hard, and when tribulation and suffering come to him, you bear that suffering with him. This type of oneness is the Christian ideal.

If the believers are the body of Christ, then could there be more than one church? There are many different denominations and kinds of Christianity, which indicates that Jesus' body has been divided up. This is not acceptable in the sight of God. It is just as though Jesus' body itself has been torn apart.

Under God there must be one further universal, substantial offering that is not divided between spirit and body.

This must be accomplished by people united together to offer a living sacrifice which can be accepted by God. In order to serve as a foundation Christianity must be united into one body. That is the first and most important condition to be achieved. The heart of Jesus Christ is grieved when he sees that his own body has been so shamefully divided. Christianity today is in the position of Jesus' body, but when there is one mind, how can there be 1,000 bodies? There should be one mind and one body.

Are all the hierarchies in Christianity really the one body of Christ? Can the Pope in Rome claim that he is completely one with Christ, and that the mind of Jesus and the body of the Pope are one? Originally God intended for the Pope to be the one symbolic body of Jesus, representing all Christians of the world.

In reality there is a gap between Jesus and the people that cannot be closed, however much they try to unite. Because Jesus' own mind and body were not sacrificed together 2,000 years ago it is impossible for Christians today to completely unite with Jesus. One more gigantic step is needed in order to complete the universal offering which was predicted, in which the body of Jesus and the mind of Jesus are totally united to become the living sacrifice on the altar.

Jesus came to unite everything into one through his sacrifice. You must understand one thing very clearly: when Jesus came as a living sacrifice, should he have come down to unite with the people, or should the people have gone up to unite with him as the sacrifice?

Would you ask Jesus to come to you, promising that you would faithfully wait for him, or would you say, "Lord, you just sit right there. I will dash to where you are?" We are the ones to move and take action. This is what God and Jesus are expecting of us. Jesus did not say that he would do our repenting for us and then bring the Kingdom of Heaven to us while we sat still. He said, "Repent, for the Kingdom of Heaven is at hand!" We are the ones who must adapt. Jesus did not come to be changed; we are the ones to be changed.

This point must be absolutely clear.

Think of your situation the same way that Jesus thought about his. In walking through the valleys of Israel Jesus did not think of them as belonging to someone else. He thought, "God is my God. Israel is my nation. These are my people." There was always an intense seriousness in his heart. Are you of the same frame of mind? Are you thinking, "God is my God. Humankind are my people, and I am here to save them?"

What was the conviction and philosophy of Jesus? Did he just routinely eat good meals and idly pass his days, planning to live a long life? Jesus thought, "God is my God. Humankind are my brethren, and this whole world is waiting to be re-created by the Son of God. I am here for that mission." God thought in the same way Jesus did.

Jesus has wanted to give his inheritance to the Christian world, to his brothers and sisters. He has wanted to give each Christian the conviction, "God is my God, humankind are my brothers and sisters. This land belongs to me and I am responsible to God to re-create it in God's way." Those denominational and sectarian leaders only interested in promoting their own sectarian purposes are so wrong. We must inherit Jesus' philosophy and idealogy instead. Denominationalism is just a roadblock for God. We must break away all the barriers of sectarianism in order to really reach the people.

If the ministers and clergy who preach sermons on Sunday morning cannot talk about God as "my God," or about humankind as "my people," or about this world as the home of one human family, they are heretics. They are frauds if they cannot talk with conviction about these things.

Who are you then? Do you feel that God is "my God"? Beyond the boundary of America, have you thought about all lands belonging to you? Have you ever thought, "I am responsible for this land. I have to invest myself in restoring this land in the sight of God"? This is the kind of religion God has been waiting for. We must feel totally responsible, as if this world belonged to us, for nobody else will take care of it. "I must take up responsibility because the churches are crumbling today. The young people are morally corrupted so I must take up the responsibility. I can see the world crumbling because of the infiltration of communism, and so I must be responsible for communism." We each have to think in this way.

When you lie down you must think that you are Jesus lying down: "My body is the resurrected body of Jesus. I am reviving Jesus' breath that was stilled 2,000 years ago." Is this criminal in light of the Bible? Not at all. The Bible is teaching us to become one body with Jesus; Jesus taught, "I am in the Father and the Father is in me." He also said, "You are in me and I am in you." Jesus meant that everyone can become a representative of the Messiah, a part of the Messiah. Your becoming the physical manifestation of the Messiah is the essence of God's ideology and Jesus' ideology. God created everyone to be a messiah. As long as there are people who need to be saved the title of Messiah is needed.

4

Christianity
In Crisis

From Jesus Christ a new world of salvation could be established. That is the history of Christianity. It went through the same course as Jesus. Whenever Christianity went to a strange country for the first time, the men and women who went with it had to undergo difficulties and shed their blood. Those who died undertook such suffering in order to be separated from the world and from Satan. They stood in the position where they could receive God's love and make themselves a sacrifice for others. If they had wanted to curse those who killed them, there could have been no providence for restoration. They had to pray for those who killed them. Without that kind of mind Christianity couldn't proceed in the manner it did. Those things occurred because God had the intention to forgive Adam and Eve after they fell, if only an unfallen brother and sister would have come out to console God's painful mind, think of the pain of their fallen brother and sister, and sacrifice themselves for the sake of the other.

All through human history, offerings have been sustaining the providence of God. In the Old Testament Age they made the offering of animals, but in the New Testament Age, Jesus Christ himself was in the place of the offering. Jesus was the "substantial offering," who labored hard in utter obedience to God and sacificed himself. So, in that situation, all humankind had to be united into one with Jesus and, by placing themselves in the position of Jesus, had to go through the offering. If, in his career in God's providence, Jesus had succeeded in saving all humankind both spiritually and physically, then we could have been saved on both levels too; but he left salvation in the physical realm unaccomplished and accomplished salvation only in the spiritual realm. Since we are with him, it means we have realized salvation only in the spiritual realm.

By the crucifixion Jesus lost his base in the physical world—his physical body. So the purpose of Christianity is also to restore that lost physical body of Jesus. But Christianity cannot realize this goal without restoring the land, the people and the sovereignty. Christians have to stand in the position where they can fulfill the providence of sacrifice on the levels of society, nation and world. In other words, Christians have to resolve to offer themselves as sacrifices.

After Jesus' crucifixion and glorious resurrection, the Christian church spread throughout Asia Minor. The principal thrust was toward Rome. Rome was the target because at that time Rome was "the world." For the world to be saved Rome had to be conquered by the army of Jesus Christ. But this was an impossible battle, an inconceivable goal. The Roman Empire appeared as an impregnable fortress not subject to conquest. Jesus' army was barehanded. They used no weapons, neither swords nor spears. They were armed only with their love of God and Jesus Christ. They marched fearlessly onward, in conviction and strength. They paid the price in blood and sacrifice.

There can be no stronger army than the one which does

not fear death. No enemy is invincible against an army of
faith. History is witness to the deeds of that army of Jesus.
The Roman Empire fell at last, and Jesus conquered Rome.
Roman Catholicism became the center of God's dispensation for world salvation. The Pope was in the position to
become God's champion.

However, in the Middle Ages, corruption appeared in the
church, and Christianity declined in spirit. Medieval church
officials often were interested in their own power, their own
authority, and their own welfare. The church enjoyed formidable power both politically and economically. The hierarchy preserved this power, abused this power, and forgot
about God's purpose. Church leaders clung tenaciously to
their positions and ruthlessly persecuted their opponents.
The hierarchy claimed lineage from Jesus' disciples, yet
they could not rise above their own sins. The Christian
spirit in many of these men was absolutely dead.

But God had to continue forward. He is never satisfied
with less than a total response. In medieval times when
there was much corruption in society, people like St. Francis denied everything and retreated from the world. Instead
of pursuing worldly goals he was loyal to a vision that he
must revitalize the spirit of the church. He started a
movement to enable Christians to give up those things
which enslaved them, and gave everything toward that goal.
By overcoming worldly things he could greatly advance and
also lead everyone who understood his goal. However, even
the Franciscan Order became a dissent-ridden organization.
The church needed more profound reform, so religous
revolution came. Martin Luther sparked the Protestant
Reformation, and significant reformers emerged within the
Catholic ranks as well. Throughout Europe, righteous people determined to win liberation from the confinement of
outmoded and abusive doctrines and practices. They
wanted to worship God and Jesus, not the church as a
worldly institution. The priesthood of all believers was the
Protestant proclamation. Direct communication with God
was their true desire. They helped God bring the world step

by step closer to the ultimate goal.

Later in England, many people objected to and resisted the autocratic practices of the state church. There was an outcry for extensive reform of the Church of England. The Puritan movement began, and it quickly spread even amid persecution. These new seekers were a threat to the established church leaders, who used almost any means to suppress the new movement. Those who truly wanted freedom of worship soon had either to flee or to be imprisoned. Their spirit was strong, but they did not have enough power to resist the government at that time. They fled to Holland. And still they longed for some new world, some new heaven and new earth where they could find freedom to worship God.

America must have seemed attractive to those who were dreaming of a new world. Even though America was unknown territory, it promised them the freedom of worship they craved. The Pilgrims strongly desired to create a community of their own. America seemed an ideal place, so they made the courageous decision to venture there. They committed themselves to the treacherous journey across the Atlantic. They risked their very lives, finding strength in their faith, which was stronger than their desire for life itself.

Think of it: They had to give up their families, their relatives, their surroundings, and their country, and head toward an unknown land. Their only hope was in God. Every step they took they depended upon God. Their journey was long, and there were many storms. They prayed unceasingly to God. They had but one way to turn. They turned to God. When they were sick and dying on the voyage, they had no medicine to take, no doctor to care for them; they turned to God. Those Pilgrim men and women were one with God. And that is how they survived.

Put yourself in their position of total reliance on God. What a wonderful faith! I am sure that the faith of the Pilgrims touched the heart of God. And when God is moved He offers promises; and when He makes promises,

He will fulfill them. God determined to give these faithful people the ultimate thing they wanted—freedom of worship. He then determined to give them even more.

I am sure you know, as I have learned, that the Mayflower arrived at Plymouth Rock in New England almost in the dead of winter. November in New England is rather cold. The destiny of the newcomers could have been only starvation because there was so little food to eat. Given this fact, it really inspires me to learn about the store of grain in the hold of the Mayflower which they would not touch, even though they were starving to death. They preserved this grain for planting the next spring. This was truly a supreme example of sacrifice. They preferred to die hoping in tomorrow rather than to act in desperation for only a few more days of life.

The Pilgrims came to this land full of purpose and hope. They knew that this purpose of theirs was more important than preserving their own lives. Nothing could have given them this courage, this dedication, this sacrificial spirit except their faith in God. When they arrived at Plymouth Rock, the forty one men who had survived the voyage got together and organized their ideas for government. The resulting Mayflower Compact was signed, "In the Name of God, Amen." This is really a wonderful story. This little group of people left Europe with their hope set in God. They grew sick and died in God; they survived in God. They formed their first government and signed their official papers, "In the Name of God."

The story of the Pilgrims is a classic in God's history. It fits into the pattern of the righteous people of history, such as Abraham, Isaac, and Moses. These Pilgrims were the Abrahams of modern history. They therefore had to brave many hardships even after the Mayflower Compact was signed.

During the first winter in America, the population of the hardy Mayflower survivors was cut in half. Each day that winter brought a heartbreaking separation from loved ones. One by one these courageous pioneers died. Yet their life from morning to night, from dusk to dawn, was centered upon the will of God. God was their only comfort, their only hope and their only security. God was the principal Partner for them. Here was an example of such a rare and pure group of God's people. They demonstrated untiring faith, and God gave them power and courage. They never lost their trust in God and their vision of the future. Their purpose in coming to America was to build a commonwealth centered on God, to establish the land where God could dwell, where they could really share fellowship with each other and rejoice in fellowship with God. This was all in God's providence, because He needed a Christian nation to serve as His champion for the ultimate and permanent salvation of the world.

So another miracle came to the Pilgrims. When they were just barely surviving and their population had been halved, the native Americans could easily have wiped them out with one stroke. But again, God was a shield for them. The first group the Mayflower survivors encountered was not hostile. They in fact welcomed the settlers. How are we to interpret this? God intervened to save His people here in America. This is my belief. God wanted them to settle, and He gave the Pilgrims a chance.

As the population of the settlement grew, they ultimately pushed native peoples away to enlarge their own colony. Of course, this land did not belong to the new American people originally. The land already possessed inhabitants, and the Pilgrim settlers were invaders from that point of view. Why then did God give these settlers their great chance? Here is my interpretation: God sided with the settlers because it was in His plan. In addition, these Pilgrims met God's requirements and truly demonstrated an unwavering faith in God. God could not help but give them His promise and fulfill that promise.

America's existence was according to God's providence. God needed to build one powerful Christian nation on earth for His future work. After all, America belonged to God first, and only after that to the people who lived here. This is the only interpretation that can justify at all the position of the Pilgrim settlers. And it implies that if the American nation which came from the Pilgrims does not fulfill God's hope, great judgement will fall on behalf of the native Americans.

This continent was hidden away for a special purpose and was not discovered by European Christians until the appropriate hour. The people of God came at the appointed hour. They came to mold the new way of life. Their principal Partner was God. At home, in caring for their children, in farming or cooking or building, they let God share their work. He was the only security they had. A farmer might dedicate his family and his farm to God, sealed with prayer around the hearth and in the fields. Their everyday life was lived in the name of God.

After the first spring visited them, they cleared the fields, planted, cultivated, and harvested the crop. And they attributed all their harvest to the grace of God. The beautiful tradition of Thanksgiving thus originated. Following the next severe winter, the first thing they built was a church. The first road they built was the road to the church. At night, at dawn, in the morning and at noontime, they prayed to God. I am sure they prayed, "God, we want to build a place for You which must be better than the Old World. We want to build a place where You can dwell and be master."

And they also had a vision that in the future this Christian nation would do more good for the rest of the world than any other country upon the face of the earth. I am sure that after their church they built a school. They wanted outstanding schools for their children, better than any schools existing in the Old World. And their homes came last. After they built these homes, they dedicated them to God. This is the legacy of your ancestors, I know. I can visualize early America as a beautiful America, because God was dwelling everywhere. In the school, in the church, in the kitchen, in the street—in any assembly or market place, God was dwelling.

I understand that in America you are approaching your nation's 200th birthday. Let us examine the people who led the independence movement in this country in 1776. Those freedom fighters were traitors in the eyes of the British Crown. But God could use these traitors as His instruments, as His people, and through them He conceived and built the best nation upon the face of the earth.

George Washington, Commander-in-Chief of the Continental Army, tasted the bitterness of defeat in many, many battles. When he finally faced the last heartbreaking winter at Valley Forge, he was serious. I am sure George Washington prayed like this: "God, it is You who led our people out of Europe and brought us over here to the New World; You don't want us to repeat the history of Europe. You liberated us and gave us freedom. You don't want to see the mistakes in Europe repeated in this land. Let me give you my pledge. I will *build one nation under God*." Thus George Washington made his battle God's battle, and therefore the victory won was a victory for God.

I know that this victory and the independence of America came because God accepted George Washington's prayer, along with the prayers of many other Americans. God knew that His champions would work for His new nation. But George Washington had nothing to work with, and the British army had everything—power, authority, tradition, and equipment. They were proud of their military strength. The American Continental Army had no ammunition and few soldiers. George Washington finally had one weapon only: Faith in God. I believe that George Washington's position paralleled David's in his fight against the giant Goliath. David won his battle in the name of the Lord. George Washington won his battle in the name of God. They both let God vanquish their foe. Each of them put his whole heart, his whole being, his whole sacrificial spirit into the battle, and won.

It is a significant fact that throughout history, God's people could never be blessed on their own homeland. God moves them out of their homeland and settles them on foreign soil, and there they can become a people and a nation of God. True to this pattern, the American people journeyed in faith out of their homelands, came across the ocean to the New World, and here received God's blessing. God had a definite plan for America. He needed to have this nation prosper as one nation under God. With God, nothing is impossible. So out of the realm of impossibility the independence of America became a fact, and upon its foundation, great prosperity came.

The British army fought for their king. For them, the British Crown was supreme. The American army fought for their King. God was their only King, and He alone was supreme. The New World was pioneered in the name of God. America is called "the land of opportunity." Here is the soil on which people find opportunity in God.

The Christian tradition in America is a most beautiful thing for foreigners to behold when they come to this country. I learned that every day your Congress is convened in prayer. Your President is sworn into office by putting his hand on the Bible. One day I visited a small prayer room in your Capitol building. When your leaders have grave decisions to make, they come to this place, kneel humbly before God and ask His help. There is a stained glass window depicting George Washington on his knees in prayer. Here I saw the true greatness of America. From the highest echelons of Congress way down to the rustic customs of the countryside, evidence of dependence upon God can be seen everywhere in America.

In this respect America is a unique nation. Even your money, the bills and coins, are impressed with such a beautiful inscription, "In God We Trust." No other nation does such a thing. Then whose money is it, your money? Is it American money? No, it is God's money. Every bill or coin says so. You are the stewards, and God has deposited His wealth in your hands. Yes, this nation is not the American nation, it is God's nation. And such a nation exists for the entire world, not just for America herself. Yes, America was formed as a new nation, a new Christian nation under a new tradition. The shackles of old traditions fell away in America. You must want to build upon this foundation a new nation under God.

God's purpose is the salvation of the world and all humankind. Today in America, therefore, you must not think that you have such wealth because you yourselves are great. We must humbly realize that the blessing of God came to America with the purpose of making it possible for God to use this nation as His instrument in saving the world. If America betrays God, where can God go? If America rejects God, where can God go to fulfill His aim? Do you want to let him try to go to the Communist world? To underdeveloped countries? God wants to have America as His base, America as His champion. And America was begun in the sacrificial spirit pursuing God's purpose. America must consummate her history in the same sacrificial spirit for God's purpose. Then America will endure forever!

Let me compare two striking examples. The people who came to America—to North America—came seeking God and freedom of worship. The dominant motive of the first settlers was God. When they came for God, they not only found God, but they also found freedom and wealth. At the same time many people went to South America. Their dominant motivation was to find gold. South America is a fertile land, no less than the North American continent. But when the colonists' motivation was gold, they could find neither gold, nor God, nor freedom. And the South American countries remain relatively underdeveloped nations.

The United States of America is the miracle of modern history. You have built the most powerful nation in history in a short time. Was this miracle possible only because you worked hard? Certainly you did work hard. However, hard work is not explanation enough. If God had not been the principal Partner, creating today's America would have been impossible. God played a prime role in American history, and this He wants America to know.

Then what has made America prosperous like this? What

made it so? That was the Christian ideology. Without the Christian ideology you could not have united, transcending European national origins, and even the fifty states, you know, could not have accepted the federal government.

Then without Christian ideology there would have been rupture and you would have created the second Europe. Like the old world, there would have been disharmony. Before your ancestors came to this continent, there had been, in Europe, international disharmony, religious rupture, and persecution of Christian people. That's what made your ancestors flee from their own countries to settle on this continent. And their way of life was to worship God in freedom.

The time has come for the American people to be awakened. Because of the noble beginning of this country, God sent His blessing and promise. The sacrificial devotion of your ancestors was the foundation for God's blessing. If you betray your ancestors, if you betray God, there is only one way for America to go. It will go to destruction. Since America was built on the pillars of faith in God, if God is moved out of American life, your nation will be without support. Your decline will be rapid.

In the Bible it says that it is more difficult for a camel to go through the eye of a needle than for a rich person to go to Heaven. In the same way, it is as difficult for a rich nation to go to Heaven. To realize the Kingdom of Heaven on earth through American people is just that difficult. It will be easier for a poor nation, such as in South America or Africa. The only way to overcome this problem would be for you Americans to throw off the effects of all your education and sophistication and give yourself up in sacrifice for the sake of others. With that, we can have hope for North Americans; but if you want to keep everything you have and try to follow God, it won't work. If you voluntarily take on a miserable situation, maybe there is hope for you. In fact, if you did that, the Kingdom of Heaven on earth could emerge very quickly.

When we look back through history we see that God used

religion to teach people to be humble and forgiving. Christianity is distinguished from other religions in that the practice of Christian love is more advanced than any seen in history because it emphasizes forgiveness and sacrifice. Without this ideal of forgiveness and love, God could never save humankind.

When we look around the world, what religion is practicing forgiveness and love? Is Christianity now persevering, accepting and loving everything? No, most Christians have built walls around themselves, being concerned only for their own salvation. Many of today's Christians are forsaking the world and wanting to be isolated. What about God? Is He isolated from the misery of the world? Is He only concerned about a certain group of people? No, He is everywhere. Islam may be the second greatest religion in the world today but Muslims are acting the same as Christians in this matter. Many cherish their own believers and country, but do not care so much about other people and nations. Many Buddhists are the same; they never think about embracing Christians; they don't know how and they don't care. They don't go out to society and try to solve the problems of the world.

We reap as we sow. Today the world is divided into two major camps and a global struggle faces us. Why has this phenomenon occurred? History was sown in the time of Jesus. Jesus was the seed of history. His crucifixion was the sowing. There were two thieves crucified with Jesus, one on the right-hand side, and one on the left-hand side.

Since Jesus went into heaven through the cross, at the time of reaping he will return through the cross. The circumstances at the time of the crucifixion of Jesus form the pattern which will be repeated on the global scale at the time of his return. And that time is now.

Today, we are aware that Communism is a strong force in this world. The Communists say, "There is no God." And the democratic world or free world says, "God exists." Why do we call the democratic faction in politics "right," and the Communist faction "left"? Where did this terminology come from? There is an ultimate reason seen from the providential perspective we have been pursuing. This terminology was determined at the time of Jesus' crucifixion. The thief crucified on Jesus' right side foreshadowed the democratic world, and the thief crucified on Jesus' left side represented the Communist world.

The thief on the left side condemned Jesus even on the cross, saying, "Are you not the Christ? Save yourself and us!" (Luke 23:39) He was saying: If you really were the Son of God, you would come down and save yourself and save me. Jesus was silent. He did not answer the man. There was also a defender of Jesus, the thief on the right. He said to the thief on the left, "Do you not fear God, since you are under the same sentence of condemnation? And we indeed justly; for we are receiving the due reward of our deeds; but this man has done nothing wrong." (Luke 23:40-41)

What faith was shown by this man on the right-hand side of the cross! He forgot his own death and defended Jesus. What a noble deed. And Jesus responded: "Truly, I say to you, today you will be with me in Paradise." (Luke 23:43)

At that moment the seed was sown by the left-hand side thief that the God-denying world would come into being: the Communist world of today is such a world. And the seed for the existence of a God-fearing world was sown by the thief on the right-hand side. The free world is in the position of the right-hand side thief. And America is the center of those God-fearing free world nations. America has been chosen as the defender of God, whereas Communism says to the world, "There is no God."

The Renaissance began the trend of human thinking which in effect kicked God out of the universe; human beings wanted to feel that they didn't need God. Now five hundred years later we can see that from Satan's point of view that trend was very successful in chasing God out of the world. Today people are trying to oust religion altogether. Those people who believed in God used to have great dignity, but now they are the object of ridicule and derision. Things are totally upside down. Christianity has been backed into a corner by the ungodly ideology of communism, which sneers, "Show me God and then I will believe." But Christians have no way to show God because they are not sure themselves.

Communists are completely confident they can take over churches and use them as their tools. They are distributing money to their members who are to become faithful church attendees. They appear to be absolutely devout Christians and give lots of money to the church and through this they may control the pastor, the church administration and sometimes actually infiltrate as pastors themselves. These young people revealed that many communist priests, pastors and ministers have already infiltrated into various church hierarchies.

Communists are promoting Christianity because one day they want to utilize Christianity to set up a revolution. The churches have the kind of atmosphere that allows them to become instruments for an ultimate communist takeover. This is what is happening today. In Korea there are many Christians who maintain a policy which helps Communists. In the name of Christianity and human rights, they are trying to tear down the anti-communist posture and discredit such leadership. These priests are proclaiming that Jesus Christ was the first communist because he blessed the poor and chastised the rich. The Communists are wolves in sheep's clothing.

One day Communists will use Christian churches as their bases of operation. This is the reality happening right now in America. A principal Communist tactic is division. They set up division everywhere; when they infiltrate Christianity they will make division between Judaism and Christianity. Communists now are uniting Judaism and Christianity, both Protestant and Catholic, to oppose the Unification Church. When this plan has succeeded they will move to the next step, and after dividing Judaism and Christianity they will pit them against each other.

The Christian churches thus have become a stage for some who don't even believe in God. The confusion evidenced by the "God is dead" theology has entered the mainstream of Christianity. Christians who follow such leaders are greatly confused now, and turn to God, asking, "Where are You, God? Answer me. I am helpless." But there seems to be no answer. Meanwhile the God-denying people appear to be showing a great deal of confidence and enthusiasm, talking about utopia and heaven on earth.

The tug of war that started with Cain and Abel has today expanded to the worldwide level. God is pulling His world and Satan is pulling his world; God is pulling Abel and Satan is pulling Cain. The dispensation of Cain and Abel is for the younger to achieve the position of the elder, and the elder to take the position of the younger. This process of restoring the birthright must be fulfilled from the individual scale up by stages to the worldwide scale. God has been winning through heavenly struggle, slowly fitting things back into their original order. Through the process of reversal God started His work at the far end, bringing everything back to its consummation at the center.

The religious world of today is in the position of Abel, the younger brother, while the non-religious world is in Cain's position. Cain will always seek to persecute Abel, and throughout history the religious world has always been persecuted. Cain always claims that Abel must submit to him. Always the satanic world takes the initiative to suppress the religious world, and always there is struggle.

It is America's position to say to the Communists, "What are you talking about? God exists. God dwells right here, with us." Is America taking this position? No! Today's America is quickly turning self-centered and away from God. America doesn't seem to care about the rest of the world. But you must give America to the rest of the world as a champion of God. When America helped others, sent out missionaries and more aid to starving people, she enjoyed her golden age. Confrontation with Communism could be done from a position of strength at that time.

But today America is retreating. It is not just an accident that great tragedy is constantly striking America and the world, such as the assassinations of President Kennedy and Dr. Martin Luther King, and the sudden deaths of Secretary-General Hammarskjold of the United Nations and Pope John XXIII, all in the same decade. The spirit of America has declined since then. Unless this nation, unless the leadership of this nation, lives up to the mission ordained by God, many troubles will plague you. God is beginning to leave America. This is God's warning.

In our time, all Christians should be world champions, destined to fulfill for God the role of the right-hand side thief. Christians must rise and be willing to struggle for the salvation of the world. But Christians today are too busy perfecting their separate denominations and church interests. We must unite with the coming of the Lord. The end of the world signifies that the time of the arrival of the Lord of the Second Advent is near. He must have a base somewhere, some foundation prepared upon which he can begin to fulfill his mission. God knew that the second Messiah would need a new environment. For that purpose God worked for 2,000 years to set up one landmark achievement, the creation of democracy. Here in America you have a democracy which upholds rights guaranteed by the Constitution, including the rights of free speech, assembly and freedom of religious belief. That was God's most important preparation for the coming of the Messiah. If this nation did not guarantee religious rights, could I freely preach like this? Would I be safe in this country? Even with its democracy there has been some religious martyrdom in America. America is meant to be that base for God's will to progress today, but America is deeply troubled.

Christians today are still a minority in the world. Are they respected by the rest of the population? Christians have become arrogant, feeling that they are especially privileged people of God and the rest of the world is doomed to die. Many Christians believe that when Jesus comes again they will be lifted up to meet the Lord in the air while the rest of the world is consumed in the fire of judgement. How can the rest of the world admire people like that?

When I first came to America, I went to New York and stood on Fifth Avenue during the rush hour. Suddenly tears began pouring down my face. I looked at the wonder of the Empire State Building and the magnificence of the new Trade Center—the tallest buildings in the world. But I asked myself, "Does God dwell in those buildings?"

New York is becoming more and more a city without God. It is a city of crime. Such a beautiful city is now crumbling. I can see so much immorality and so many signs of godlessness in that city. It was shocking to my eyes as I stood watching during that rush hour. I could see so many things at once that are all intolerable in the sight of God.

I asked God, "Is this the purpose for which you blessed America?" I know God wants to see His spirit prevail in those great buildings. In those beautiful automobiles He wants to see young people strong in their enthusiasm for God and the love of others. It doesn't take the Empire State Building to glorify God; it doesn't take a new automobile to glorify God. Even if you have only a rock as your altar, when you pour out your hope and your tears upon it for the service of God, God is with you. I can really see that God is leaving the great city of New York. New York is instead becoming the city of evil.

America has been known as the "melting pot" where people of all colors, creeds, and nationalities are melted into one new breed. In order to melt anything, heat is required. Do you know who provided the heat for America? God was that heat. Without God, you could never have melted your people together.

America could only achieve true brotherhood through the Christian spirit, but when you begin to lose this foundation, America's moral fiber will deteriorate. Today there are many signs of the decline of America. What about the American young people? What about your drug problems and your juvenile crime problems? In the time of Jesus leprosy was a great problem; drugs are the leprosy of America today. Young people are being corrupted by the use of LSD, heroin, and other drugs. Red China manufactures opium for export to other countries. They smuggled drugs into Vietnam, where American soldiers were fighting against Viet Cong. When the soldiers were discharged, they brought back drugs. Sold in the United States, the heroin earned ten times what they paid for it. In the past, England exported opium to China and India to corrupt their youth. Now, Red China is using the same strategy to corrupt Western youth, and Western youth show no resistance.

If you become a drug user, however hard you may struggle you cannot get rid of the habit. You need money for your habit. You'll do anything to get the money. America loses billions of dollars a year through its drug problem. The other day I learned that 92 percent of the American Unification Church members had been drug users before they joined our movement. We can imagine that almost all young people use drugs. In Germany the Nazis killed six million Jewish people. But young people are being killed in larger quantities by drugs. If we let it go on as it is, it will spread out to every person, it will corrupt the whole nation. The Communists working underground in this nation, are they using drugs? No, they forbid their youth to use drugs. It is their weapon to use drugs to corrupt the young people of the free world.

What about the breakdown of your families? I hear that one out of every two marriages in America end in divorce. The California state government is issuing more divorce certificates than marriage licenses. What about the glut of pornography littering your society? Some twenty five thousand children disappear or are abandoned every year in America. Many come to brutal ends to satisfy the appetites of child pornographers, for the sake of lust and money. The tone of your national entertainment media reflects this rapid disappearance of moral sense from America.

American society has degenerated to such an extent that it is making Sodom and Gommorah look trivial. The "gay liberation" movement is gaining tremendous momentum, but that is virtually a tool of Satan by which he seeks to destroy the most precious, fundamental values of God. The gay movement seeks to justify itself through gaining legal, political and ultimately moral power, but this is disgusting in the sight of God.

The word, "sin," refers to violation of the law of the love of God. God abhors sin, and the misuse of love is the crime God abhors the most. Ultimately the law and love of God will prevail. Therefore, whoever indulges in unprincipled love can only perish. America today is no exception to this rule; it must not violate the law of the love of God or it too will be destroyed. It was because of an unchaste relationship of love that the fall occurred. We can say that the last days predicted by the Bible will be the time when selfish, individualistic love reaches its perfection. In such a world, anything other than individualistic love is scorned. There is no room for the love of country, love of humanity, and certainly no room for the love of God.

Such a trend began in the adult world but it has now come down to the realm of teenagers. That is why we have the so-called "me generation." You can see that this is happening in today's society; thus you know that we have come to the end of this world. There is virtually no way of controlling the promiscuous immorality of many of today's young people. Parents cannot control them; teachers are powerless, and society cannot do anything either. Certainly the nation and world have no power to control them.

Satan's ultimate goal is to destroy any ideal form of love while God is working to lead humankind toward the ideal, wholesome form of love. Those who are the most susceptible to Satan's temptations are Americans. The U.S.A. is the central nation for the Christian culture, yet at the same time this nation has become morally degraded, particularly in love.

What about racial problems? If we really love the world, can there be segregation between white and yellow and black? There is no question but that this is impossible. Thus, in the sight of God America must be ashamed. That there is a problem in this country between white and black shows that Christianity has been a failure in this country, where we find white-oriented churches and black-oriented churches. When the new universal age comes, a nation pursuing a racist course will be a failure. And what about the persistent problems of poverty in the world's wealthiest nation? Why are all these problems occurring? These are signs that God is leaving America. I can read the sign which says, "God is leaving America now!" If this trend continues, in a very short time God will be with you no longer. God is leaving America's homes. God is leaving your culture. God is leaving your schools. God is leaving your churches. God is leaving America. There are many signs of atheism in this once God-centered nation: There have been many laws enacted that only a godless society could accept. There was a time when prayer was America's daily diet. Today you hear prayers in American schools no longer.

The reason why Americanism will never succeed is that the basic attitude here is humanism and pragmatism. Pragmatism is being very destructive because it is interested only in bringing some kind of profit to a situation, and that profit is more often centered upon material than spiritual values. This is the core problem with America today. Neither humanism nor pragmatism can help America find God's will.

I know that if I expected secular America to understand these things, I would be too naive. This culture is saturated with humanism and pragmatism and it has known virtually no other way of thinking. Naturally I will be denounced by this culture. Americans want to hear something nice about their country, but I cannot say it. I don't care whether they hate me or not—I must tell the truth. If you want to hear good words then you must live up to them.

You may want to ask, "Who are you to say these things to the American people?" Then please tell me who is taking responsibility for this country. The future of America depends upon the young people, and the churches and national institutions are failing to inspire American youth in a righteous way. We need a spiritual revolution in America. A revolution of heart must come to America.

Individualism must be tied into God-centered ideology. Who is going to do this? Who is going to kindle the hearts of American youth? Will the President do this? Will wealthy American businessmen do this? Will American churches do this?

God does not even want to look at Satan's world; Christianity, however, without knowing God's strict standard of love, is for the most part degenerating into an institution for social functions, dancing and drinking, easily accepting the rapidly declining standards of love. America needs to repent. Famous theologians, scholars, ministers, and all Americans must repent together. Recently my wife and I received some philosophers and theologians at East Garden. One Harvard Ph.D said to me, "I am a Moonie. What can I do for you?" He may have expected me to say he was a scholar and to send him traveling to speak and receive glory, but I told him to be a lightning rod and receive more persecution than Jesus received, for the sake of the young people of this nation, even if he should falter and die. I told him if he did that then people would heap unending honors upon his tomb. Was that a cruel statement or a great blessing?

We must restore God-centered morality or else America is destined to collapse. The Roman Empire collapsed from within, of its own moral corruption, not from outside attack or infiltration. America is in far worse shape than the Roman Empire was because there is no tradition left in this nation. Once the moral center is removed from America it will collapse and no trace of it will be left. America is a predominantly Christian nation yet most people in this nation don't know where they are. They are not sure about democracy or about their religion, and they are not sure about the future. Usually, when the young people within a society are in a state of confusion the older people can guide them from the standpoint of tradition. But this is no longer the case. Older people are equally as confused as the young people.

I know that God sent me here to America. I did not come

here for the luxurious life in America. Not at all! I came to America not for my own purposes, but because God sent me. For 6,000 years God has been working to build this nation. The future of the entire world hinges on America. God has a very great stake in America. Somebody must come to America and stop God from leaving.

My followers in Korea bade me farewell in tears. I know there are still many things to do in Korea. But working with only Korea would delay world salvation. America must be God's champion. I know clearly that the will of God is centered upon America. I came from Korea, I gave up my surroundings, just as many people have in the history of God's providence. I did not come to this country to make money. When I came to America, I committed my fortune, my family, and my entire life to America. I came to a new country where I can serve the will of God.

If in the midst of decline in the Christian world there sprouts up one group which thinks dearly of the love relationship between humankind and God and would be ready to sacrifice themselves for the salvation of humankind, that's the religion God would be using as His instrument. Seen from God's point of view, too, God would want a group of Christians who would set the goal of higher dimension where they teach divine love in life. If that kind of group is found, the Christian world will never perish, but there will be reanimation and revitalization, bringing it back to life.

Many Christians always talk about being saved so that they can have their little niche in heaven. Too many of them don't care about the world or about loving people. They don't want to waste their energy on the world. But heaven is not a place. Heaven is love. Unless you perfect your love, and unless you possess God's ideal and practice it on earth, don't talk about heaven. Is there corruption in the Christian world in America? Are people glad over the fact or sad? Most people feel freedom, and they leave the church and then they feel as though they are liberated. It's a sign of peril coming to the United States. Unless there come together people who will do something to change America and the world, there's no hope for the world to be changed or saved. In other words, we need a stronger Christian group with a stronger ideology, because all other ways have been proven to be failures. If, maybe, black people emerge with a stronger leadership than others, we must be able to follow them. You must follow the leadership and you must realize the bitter fact that the desire of the Communist world or the satanic world in general is to destroy this world of religion, the world in which people believe in God. So the first target for the satanic power is Christianity, and their final target within Christianity is the family, which is the core of divine love.

Where do you think Christianity has been ruined? Right here in America. It has become apathetic and compromised itself and you cannot avoid judgement for that. America is the nation that reduced Christianity to a trivial religion. There are hundreds of millions of Christians around the world and millions in America alone. All of those people could easily save America, yet they have allowed this nation to be influenced by communism and become degraded morally, remaining totally selfish. They should feel so ashamed about this that they cannot lift up their faces. Jesus taught that Christians should take up the cross.

The United States has been prepared by God as the foundation for God's will. The rich natural resources of this country, as I see it, do not belong first to American citizens—they belong first to God, and they are placed here for God's will to be done. Because the founding ideology of this nation is Christianity, and Christianity is the foundation to inherit God's heart, God blessed this nation centering on Christian people. It was not only so the people of the United States could enjoy wealth that God blessed them. It was to unite the people of the world into one in God's love, through exchanging material goods as expressions of love. If this powerful nation should lose God's love, God's abundant material blessing will be taken away and given to the nation whose people are receiving God's love.

As I walk on the streets, I see many churches standing high as the symbols of God's love and Christianity. We must love this nation now more than Christians have in the past, and develop Christian culture into a world culture of higher dimension. This great ideology of democracy should be used for the whole world, but the United States is using it for the scope of Americans alone. We must help the world to be a better place in which to live, and not neglect our responsibility, as Americans are now doing.

The fundamental spirit of Christianity is to live for other people. Christianity is for the sake of the nation, something bigger than Christianity itself. If Christianity centers on itself and works for the prosperity of its own self, then it is doomed to decline. God sees Christianity as existing for the future generations and for the whole. God does not take Christianity as the most important thing, but by using Christianity as the sacrifice, He wants to save the whole world. God set up Christianity in order to save all humanity. But Christians have been living self-centered lives, and this is the sign of the decline of Christianity.

We must be humble. We must initiate from this moment the most crucial movement that could be possible, the movement to bring God back home. All of your pride, your wealth, your cars and your great cities are like dust without God. We must bring God back home. In your homes, your churches, your schools and your national life, our work for God's purpose must begin. Let's bring God back, and make God's presence in America a living reality.

I have initiated a new youth movement for the salvation of America. This is a new Pilgrim movement. Does it seem strange that a man from Korea is initiating an American youth movement for God? When you have a sick member of your family, a doctor comes from outside of your house. When your house is on fire, the fire fighters come from outside. God has a strange way of fulfilling His purpose. If there is no one in America meeting your needs, there is no reason why someone from outside cannot fulfill that role. America belongs to those who love her most.

The mere number of the Christian population in America is not impressive. You cannot impress God with numbers, but only with fervent faith. The standard is the quality of Abraham's faith. How many Christians in America are really crying out with fervor for God? How many American Christians feel that God's work is their own work? How many people put God first? How many are ready to die for God?

Somebody must begin, and begin now. Even under persecution somebody must begin. Someone must give him or herself up for the purpose of God and bring God back home. America is a Christian nation, but present-day Christianity cannot eradicate all the evil, so the established Christianity cannot finally overcome the problems; it is powerless. Indeed, it has been within Christian culture that the problems have spread so virulently. A new power, growing up within Christianity, must emerge to do the job. We must have our churches filled with fiery faith; we must create new homes where our families can be really happy, and we must finally create a new society, a new spiritual nation where God can dwell. America must go beyond America! This is the only way for this country to survive. Don't ever worry about your own heaven, but worry about bringing down the Kingdom of God to your society and to this world. If you are like that, when you say to God, "I don't want to go to the Kingdom of Heaven," God will chase after you and personally install you in the highest position in His Kingdom.

The true Christians are those who are willing to sacrifice themselves, their own church and their denomination for the fulfillment of the will of God for world salvation.

A true Christian could not pray for God's help and blessing for only his or her family. After knowing the truth of God's situation we can only pray, "God, I am ready to be Your sacrifice. Use me as Your instrument; fulfill Your will for world salvation through me. If necessary please sacrifice my family, church and nation." Such people will create the Kingdom of God.

Those who pray only for their own chunk of God's blessing will end up in hell. If God's concern is world salvation, do you think He would support the person who was interested only in himself, his family and his church, or would He side with the people who were most involved in world salvation?

Put yourself in God's position for a moment and look at the American churches. Not only are there a great many churches, but they are pursuing very different purposes and goals. White people organize together, black people organize their churches and yellow people organize their churches. Do you think this is a very beautiful thing for God to behold? Absolutely not! If any Christian leader would call for the people to unite with other races then he or she could be considered a true Christian leader among the people.

I know this clearly: This is the will of God. Therefore, I have come to America, where I become one voice crying in the wilderness of the 20th century. After World War II, the United States was supposed to be centered upon God and have an awareness that the world was moving toward the "great and terrible day of the Lord." There should have been a prevalent attitude within this country that the greatest thing was to love the world, to serve God, and to go beyond loving oneself or even one's own nation. People should have felt the inspiration to be pioneers for the great era that was soon to come. That was the vision that the United States was supposed to propagate in the world. If such an awakening had happened after World War II, the current tragic situation in America would never have occurred.

What has happened? The U.S. did not see such a vision. For forty years, this country has been moving down the path of self-indulgence and fun. Drugs have infiltrated the whole country; young people have been corrupted and turned more and more toward delinquency; free sex has become a way of life. But this has not been contained only within the United States. This country is the leader of the free world, so it has affected the world in a bad way. As

Americans try to make light of everything, wanting only to have fun in life, such an attitude has spread around the world.

People commonly say there is much freedom in America, but is there true freedom here? Here in America people talk about peace and freedom and unity, but there is no real peace and freedom here. Freedom is a fashionable word, but when you dig down to the bottom of it, people really are talking about selfishness. Today the Western world is degraded because of the abuse of freedom. True freedom comes under the law of love, with responsibility attached. Unless you as individuals live up to the law of the love of God, your destiny will be destruction. No one can violate that law and still flourish. The Bible says that if your arm or leg hinders you, cut it off. The Bible uses very severe language in matters of sin; there is no way around it. This is exactly what Jesus meant when he said, "If you want to lose your life, you preserve your life; and if you want to gain your life, you will lose it." He wanted to revolutionize the world in which people were so self-centered as to think only of themselves without minding other people. Nobody likes self-centered, arrogant people. If one is so humble as to exalt others, he or she is liked by everybody. We must be able to revolutionize the idea of individualism into altruism. This is the most important thing.

You have all undoubtedly encountered Unification Church people, whether on the streets or in your churches or neighborhoods. They probably seem to be so aggressive and ambitious; you may be tired of them, I am sure. But put yourself in these people's positions. Why are they doing this? Does it bring them any material profit? Eighty-five percent of the young people in our movement are college graduates. They are capable of earning tens of thousands of dollars a year, but instead they are working in church missions and living very sacrificial lives. Their hearts are compassionate. They have one purpose: They want to save America. They want to bring God back to America and they know that by serving the world they can save America.

These young people are working to rekindle America's spirit. America has a great tradition. All you have to do is revive it. We need a new movement of Pilgrims with a new vision. This is inevitable, because God left no alternative for America. You have no other direction to turn. The new Pilgrim movement has come—not for America alone, but for the world. In other words, the movement for world salvation must begin in this country. America is the base and when America fulfills her mission you will be eternally blessed.

This is God's hope for America. This is God's ardent hope for you. There is nowhere else to turn. When you bring God back into your home, your home will be secure. Your juvenile delinquency problem will be solved. There is no good answer to the racial problem except God. Communism will be no threat when God is made real. God will increase your wealth. This is the one way that America can save herself.

It is my deep desire, from my heart, that America will see the glorious day of renewal.

5

Judgement By God's Word

It is a long way from Korea to America, yet God has been driving me here from long ago. Unless I had something new to reveal, I would not come here to speak to you at all. Why should I come if I only were to repeat the things that you already know? I would like for you and me to spend this time together in openmindedness so that the spirit of God can speak directly into our hearts. Jesus taught in his Sermon on the Mount:

> Blessed are the poor in spirit, for theirs is the kingdom of heaven.

> Blessed are the meek, for they shall inherit the earth.

> Blessed are those who hunger and thirst for righteousness, for they shall be satisfied. (Matt. 5:3, 5, 6)

Tonight I humbly ask you to be the poor in spirit; I ask you to be the meek, and I ask you to become those who hunger and thirst for righteousness. Then we will all see the Kingdom of Heaven, and we shall all be satisfied. Now let us begin.

Christians, and Christianity itself, have a final hill to cross. Biblical prophecy states that Christians must pass through the end of the world and face the judgment of fire at the great and terrible day of the Lord. The Bible says we are going to see many extraordinary phenomena, in heaven and on earth, as the end comes near.

When Jesus promised his second coming, he conveyed a feeling of great imminence. From the day Jesus Christ ascended into heaven, Christians have been watching for his return to earth. For the last 2,000 years of history, it has been the hope of every Christian to see the returning Christ. But this extraordinary event has never occurred. Many people tired of waiting. Some finally decided that this second coming would not happen literally. They came to think, "This is just one of God's methods to keep us alert."

Not only Christianity, but many other religions of the world are predicting a certain end of the world. However, even though they predict it, they do not have a sure definition of the end of the world. Everyone makes his or her definition of the end of the world according to the founder of their own religion or denomination. Who really represents a universal understanding?

We must clarify the meaning of the end of the world as the Bible prophesies it. We must also know how the Lord will reappear when he comes in the fullness of time.

We should first of all understand that God did not create the world to end. He always intended the world of goodness to last forever. The God who does not create for eternity cannot be an almighty God. The *present* world must end, however, because the fall initiated a history of evil. The end of the world is necessary because we have not achieved

God's intended world of goodness. Instead of becoming children of goodness, we have in reality become creatures of evil.

Adam and Eve fell in the garden of Eden. They were not at that time in a position to have a full understanding of the will of God. They entered into a state of confusion and made the wrong choice. They were confronted with either obedience to God, which would have brought about the good world, or obedience to Satan, which did in fact bring about their fall. Between two clear choices, Adam and Eve made the wrong one. They brought evil into the world. God's original intention was to create His ideal world—a good and prosperous world He determined to last for eternity. But human beings fell, the good world of God ended abruptly, and human history started in the wrong direction.

The history of the world is therefore a history of evil. God sowed good seed, and He intended to harvest a good crop. But Satan stole His crop before it was ripened and reaped a harvest of evil. Human history is a crop of weeds.

Then let us examine when the end of the world will come. This is very important to us. The gospel says that in the last days God will separate the sheep from the goats. What is the difference between these two kinds of animals? Sheep recognize their master, the shepherd, while goats do not follow a shepherd. Today you know that our world is divided into two opposing camps. One is the democratic world, the other is the Communist world. Our free world says, "There is a God." We accept our shepherd. The Communist world says, "God does not exist." They deny their master. Thus the free world may be symbolized by sheep, and the Communist world by goats. At the time of the formation of these two conflicting ideological worlds, we can know we have come to the end of the world.

Another sign of the last days is flagrant immorality. Satan became Satan because of unchaste love. Love is a very formidable weapon of Satan. One must be equipped with a greater, more righteous love in order to conquer Satan.

Satan is always trying to trick people with cheap love. But heavenly love is beautiful and constructive in its sacrificial giving. Satan's love is unreliable and will last only a short time, but heavenly love is eternally unchanging.

Ultimately these two kinds of love will clash, confronting each other in the last days. America is facing the last days right now and we can see two extremes of love in this country: the carnal, dirty love of free sex and the deep-rooted, heavenly love now being proclaimed by righteous people. Secular love and heavenly love are confronting each other here in America. As the scope of satanic love becomes greater there will be more destruction. Families will break up; people will become corrupted; life will become miserable, and more people will commit suicide. But as heavenly love expands, our lives become richer. There is a line of judgement separating these two worlds of love, and you must stand on either one side or the other. You can not be in both.

The last days is the time for dividing good and evil, which are becoming steadily more confused. Even the most faithful believer in Jesus or the most righteous church on earth cannot proclaim proudly that they are absolutely separated from Satan and sin and that they are following Jesus exactly as he would have them do. No one can say they are living in perfect love in an ideal world with no suffering and tears. No church and no Christian could say such a thing.

This means that Satan exists within the churches as everywhere else; also, there is sin there as in the rest of the world. If this is true and if what church people love and hate is no different from what the rest of the world loves and hates, then there is very little difference between the world and the church. Which would Satan find more pleasure in—the church or the world? Satan likes the sins of the church more, because based upon them he can protest to God, "Look at those people in the church—they don't love others; they even hate others! They are not faithful, either. This must be my church." If the churches remain this way, they will decline into nothing at the time of the last days, along with the evil, secular world. This is the way of God; He will judge such churches before the judgement of the rest of society.

What really surprised me when I first came to America was the way Americans used the names of Jesus Christ and God as an exclamation—not to praise them, but to put them in the worst position. I wondered what people meant when they said, "Jesus Christ!" and I realized that they were describing something bad. What led to this kind of custom? What do the best words imaginable have to do with the worst things that can happen to people? Have you sometimes observed that certain Christians may be worse than people of the secular world? Those who claim they believe in God may actually be worse than those who don't—they are more egotistical, less loving and giving, etc.

The American nation is founded upon Judeo-Christian principles, yet Americans have become very individualistic. Was Jesus an individualistic person? How did Americans come to be so egotistical and individualistic when Jesus had nothing of a self-centered nature? We can come to the simple conclusion that if people really believed in Jesus they would not have become like that. Instead of believing in Jesus for Jesus' sake and for God's sake, some people believe in him for their own benefit. In other words, they use Jesus and God for their own sake. What do you think about this?

Then, what does the end of the world mean? Just what is going to end? Evil is going to end. God will put an end to all evil. Out of God's new beginning will come a new opportunity for the human race. And the goodness God intended in His original ideal can be made real. What will Jesus do when he comes? Will he come to wipe out the world? The word "judgement" is frequently misunderstood to mean that God will wipe out everything in anger. That is not the purpose of the Messiah's coming. The whole purpose is to fulfill the ideal that was left undone in the garden of Eden, to work for individual, family, social, national and world perfection. Judgement is the constructive work of God to

110

see the fulfillment of the Kingdom of God here on earth.

In the garden of Eden Adam and Eve fell into evil instead of developing their goodness. They was subjugated by Satan and became the children of sin. Therefore the Bible says, "You are of your father the devil,..." (John 8:44) If the fall had not occurred, then the true ruler would be God. But He is not today the King of this universe, because Satan is sitting upon God's throne. God has to remove all results of the human fall before He can truly reign over the world.

Now, the end of the world is the moment in history when God ends this history of evil and begins His new age. It is the crossroads of the old history of evil and the new history of good.

In light of this definition, why does the Bible predict extraordinary heavenly phenomena as signs of the end of the world? Will the things predicted really occur? The Bible says:

> Immediately after the tribulation of those days
> the sun will be darkened, and the moon will not
> give its light, and the stars will fall from heaven,
> and the powers of the heavens will be shaken.
> (Matt. 24:29)

What does this mean? What are we to expect?

First of all, please rest assured that these things will not happen literally. God will not destroy anything in the universe. God often expresses His truth in symbols and parables, and these biblical sayings will be accomplished symbolically. Second, God has no reason to destroy the universe. It is not the universe, but man and woman who have committed sin. Only we deviated from the original plan of God's creation. Why should God destroy the animals, or the plants, or anything in creation which fulfilled His purpose as He intended? God would not destroy those innocent things.

I want you to understand that when we say "end of the world," it does not mean the destruction of the physical world, but the end of the old ways and beginning of a new human era. The Bible therefore says, "A generation goes, and a generation comes, but the earth remains forever." (Eccl. 1:4) In Revelation we read: "Then I saw a new heaven and a new earth; for the first heaven and the first earth had passed away,..." (Rev. 21:1) That new heaven and new earth refers to the coming of a new history of God, a time of new dominion. After you buy a house, won't you move in your family and possessions? Then you will say that you have a new home, and you are the new master of the house. In the same way, when men of God occupy this universe, it will become a new heaven and a new earth.

We know that when winter ends, spring begins. But can we say at precisely what point spring starts? Who can pinpoint the exact instant of transition? You cannot know because the passage from one season to another takes place imperceptibly, quietly. The end of winter is similar to the beginning of spring, so there is no discernible moment of transition.

At what moment does the old day end and a new day begin? Although the change occurs in darkness, there is no doubt that we do go from one day to the next. The change is unnoticeable at first, but it is also inevitable and irrevocable. Although three billion people live on earth, not one among them can point to the exact moment when the old day passes and the new day begins. So we understand that from the human point of view we cannot always know the precise moment things happen. But God knows when winter passes into spring, and God knows when night opens into day. And God can point to the transition into new history.

Our step into new history is like a glorious dawn emerging out of the darkest night. The crossing point between good and evil is not obvious. You will not notice it when it happens, but it will definitely take place, just as surely as the sun will rise tomorrow.

Then how can we know when the end is approaching? God will not hide this moment from us; He does not suddenly bring judgment on the world without warning.

God will announce the coming of the great and terrible day through His prophets. Amos 3:7 says, "Surely the Lord God does nothing, without revealing his secret to his servants the prophets." God chooses His instrument and through him God announces His plans. This has been the case throughout Bible history.

The person to be chosen as God's prophet must be one of the people living in our evil world. But he or she must be a person of faith who can demonstrate worthiness to be used by God, showing absolute faith. To do this the person must give up all worldly success and completely separate from this evil world. He must purify himself by cutting off all evil attachments. He will not be popular in the evil world. God is absolute good and therefore the exact opposite of evil. That is why evil always persecutes a person of God.

Noah was such a man chosen by God and scorned by the evil world. God instructed Noah to build a ship. He sent Noah to the heights of a mountain instead of down by the riverside or to the seashore. God's command was so ridiculous in the eyes of the evil world that many people laughed at Noah. He was ridiculed, not because people thought him a particularly funny man, but because he followed God's instructions so faithfully. The eyes of the world could not understand the way of God. In this manner, with such implausible instructions, God could test the faith of the man he had chosen as His champion. This is what happened in Noah's day.

And at the time of Abraham it was no different. God called Abraham, the son of an idol-maker, and commanded him, "Leave your home at once!" God does not allow for any compromise. God takes a position where evil can be totally denied. In no other way can good begin.

God has said He will start a new history, in which no element of evil will remain. God demands complete response from human beings. Those who follow God's direction must begin from absolute denial of the evil world. That is why Jesus Christ taught: "He who finds his life will lose it, and he who loses his life for my sake will find it."

(Matt. 10:39) He also said, "...a man's foes will be those of his own household." (Matt. 10:36)

You may ask, what kind of message is this? This is God's way, to choose His own people and put them in a position where they will be rejected by evil. Otherwise His champion can do no good for God. From the point of view of God's standard, then, modern Christians have been having a very easy time. This is very strange, because there is no easy way indicated in Christian teaching. I wonder how many Christians are really serious about following the path of God? God's demand is absolute. It allows for no middle ground.

Let me tell you something about my background. I was raised a Christian in Korea. Christianity is the core of all religions. The reason for this is that in Christianity we teach the love and life relationship with God and the way of sacrificing ourselves for the sake of others. That's why I chose Christianity. I thought it was only too natural to draw the conclusion that in Christianity alone, and through Christianity alone, we can save the whole world, because there we are taught to have the relationship between God and ourselves based upon Jesus' divine love and life.

During the springtime of my youth I spent every day experiencing the most desperate, suffering situations in human life: labor camps, coal mining, begging, dock work, farming, fishing. I looked at every aspect of human life, even the world of prostitutes. I learned why women become prostitutes and why men go to prostitutes. I studied all the miseries of human life.

When I was a student in Tokyo, I rode on the railway looking for places where the most suffering people were living. Even on rainy days I would get off the train and go and sit on the bench beside unfortunate-looking people and make friends with them. I always thought to myself, "What if this man were my elder brother or my father and he was suffering on my account, what could I do for him?"

I observed the students at my university. They were always laughing, talking, and behaving very boisterously. I compared myself with them and thought, "Your laughter is meaningless; it has no weight. But through my silence and prayer, as I seek the solutions to life's problems, people will find hope in the future." I knew that the silly gaiety of my fellow students would pass away like a puff of smoke, but the sorrow and sadness I was sharing with the downtrodden of society would bring a new future for the world.

This is how I spent my entire youth, going to the places of poverty and misery, visiting the homes of miners and laborers. Also, I acquainted myself with middle-class people and upper-class people, even saving money and spending a week in the finest hotel. In my village, even though I had never committed a crime, people began to wonder about me and I could not move about freely or live my life freely. I was thinking of the nation and the world. Because of that, I was completely misunderstood. People would laugh at me, point their fingers at me. Once I undertook my life's mission, I encountered opposition on every level. My village opposed me, the society opposed me, and the nation opposed me. The most severe opposition came from established Christianity. Ministers and elders of the churches were pointing their fingers at me, accusing me of being a heretic, telling their parishioners, "Don't even go near Rev. Moon; he has a demon!" My relatives were mistreated simply because they were related to me. If I went to a village inn or to a restaurant, I was not welcome. I did nothing wrong and I committed no crime. All I was doing was pursuing the highest possible goal, which they could not understand.

Under such circumstances, winning a true friend and creating a small organization was not easy. But Jesus and the spiritual world was always on my side. In the early days of the Unification Church, nobody witnessed for the church. Members came through contact and guidance from the Spirit.

During the Korean War, it took me four months to travel by foot from North Korea to Pusan. In Korea men wear a kind of white pajamas. Taking four months, you cannot imagine how dirty it became; it was so dirty I put it inside out. There was no sleeping place, only open space. It was December, so it was very cold when I got to Pusan. To avoid this night coldness, I went to the military harbor for labor, because it was easier to work than sleep.

In the daytime I went to the mountains; among the trees I had a place to sleep, and time for myself. I enjoyed it. When I went to work I told interesting stories, and the workers would gather around me and bring me food. But I could not live like that all the time, so I had a small hut, hardly better than a dog house, a very simple dwelling place with mud and rocks on the walls and roof. There was no flat land where I was going to build. So I built up a slope. Where I built it there is a spring which passes through the middle of the floor. With boxes I made a temporary roof. The size of the room was about six feet long. Still I wore those four-month-old clothes. There was nowhere to put them in the laundry. In that humble situation spiritually chosen people found me. Even though I wore those clothes, they came.

Then how can we know clearly the path of God? Let us examine the history of God's providence. Today we are anticipating the end of the world. God has made previous attempts to end the evil world. For example, the time of Noah: That was a crossroads in history, when God wanted to bring an end to evil and begin the world of goodness. Noah was the central figure chosen in God's dispensation. To better understand Noah's mission and the meaning of the end of the world, we want to know more fully how the evil history began.

In the garden of Eden, God gave Adam and Eve a commandment. That commandment was the word of God. Then Satan approached and enticed them with a lie. And that lie was the word of evil. Adam and Eve were in a position to choose between the two words: The truth was on one side, and a lie was on the other. They chose the lie.

Because this was the process of the fall, at the end of the world God will give humankind truth. The words of God will come through His prophet. When people accept the words of God they will then pass from death to life, because truth leads to life. Human beings died in a lie, and in truth we will be reborn.

Therefore judgment comes by words. These words of God's judgement are revealed by His chosen prophets. This is the process of the ending of the world. Those who obey and listen to the new word of truth shall have life. Those who deny the word will continue to live in death.

God chose Noah to declare the word. Noah's announcement was, "The flood is coming. The salvation is the ark." The people could have saved themselves by listening to Noah's words. However, the people treated Noah as if he were a crazy man, and they perished—because they opposed the word of God. According to the Bible, only the eight people of Noah's immediate family became passengers on the ark. Only these eight believed, and only these eight were saved.

God had said to Noah, "I have determined to make an end of all flesh; for the earth is filled with violence through them; behold. I will destroy them with the earth." (Gen. 6:13) Did this actually happen? We know the evil people perished, but was the physical world demolished in the process? No. This passage was not literally fulfilled, and God did not destroy the earth. God did eradicate the people and abolish evil sovereignty, leaving only the good people of Noah's family. This was God's way to begin to restore the original world of goodness through Noah.

If God had fully consummated His restoration at that time, then we would have heard no more about the end of the world. Once the perfect world of goodness is realized, another end of the world is not necessary. Nothing could interfere with the eternal reign of God's perfect kingdom.

But the very fact that we anticipate the end of the world today is proof that the providence did not thus succeed at the time of Noah. What happened to Noah after the flood should be fully explained, but I cannot spend too much time on that subject tonight. To make a long story short, once again, sin crept into Noah's family through his son, Ham. God's flood judgment was thereby nullified, and evil human history continued, leading to the time of Jesus Christ.

With the coming of Christ, God again attempted to end the world. Jesus came to start the Kingdom of Heaven on earth. Thus, the first words Jesus spoke were, "Repent, for the kingdom of heaven is at hand." Indeed, the time of Jesus Christ's ministry was the time for the end of the world. That great and terrible day was prophesied by Malachi, about 400 years before the birth of Jesus:

> For behold, the day comes, burning like an oven,
> when all the arrogant and all evil-doers will be
> stubble; the day that comes shall burn them up,
> says the Lord of hosts, so that it will leave them
> neither root nor branch. (Mal. 4:1)

Was the judgement of Jesus Christ done by literal fire? Did the day come at the time of Jesus when everything literally turned to ashes? No, we know it did not. Since these things prophesied did not literally happen at that time, some people say that such prophecy must have been meant for the time of the Second Advent. But this cannot be the case.

John the Baptist came to the world as the last prophet; Jesus said: ". . . all the prophets and the law prophesied until John." (Matt. 11:13) The coming of John the Baptist should have brought to a close prophecy and the Mosaic Law. This is what Jesus said would happen. The purpose of all prophecy before Jesus was to prepare for his coming, and to indicate what was to be fulfilled up to the time of his coming. These prophecies are not for the time of the Lord at the second advent. God sent His son Jesus into the world, intending full salvation of spirit and flesh to be accomplished. The second coming was made necessary only by lack of consummation at the time of the first coming.

Why then was the time of Jesus the time for the end of the world? We already know the answer. It is because Jesus came to end evil sovereignty and bring forth God's sovereignty upon the earth. This was the end of the Old Testament Age and the beginning of the age of the New Testament. Jesus brought the new words of truth.

How did the people receive the gospel which he brought? They did not receive and honor his teachings. They were prisoners to the letter of the Old Testament and could not perceive the presence of the spirit of God in the new revelation. It is ironic that Jesus fell victim to the very prophecies that were to testify to him as the Son of God. By the letter of the Mosaic Law he was judged an offender. Blindly his teachings and love were rejected.

At the time of Jesus many learned people, many religious leaders and many people prominent in society who were well-versed in the Law and the Prophets were waiting for a Messiah. How happy they would have been to have their Messiah recite the Old Testament exactly, syllable by syllable and word by word! But Jesus Christ did not come to repeat the Mosaic Law. He came to pronounce a new commandment of God. People missed the whole point. And Jesus was accused. His opponents said to him, "We stone you for no good work, but for blasphemy; because you, being a man, make yourself God." (John 10:33)

The Bible states: "And they reviled him [one of Jesus' disciples], saying, 'You are his disciple, but we are disciples of Moses. We know that God has spoken to Moses, but as for this man, we do not know where he comes from.' " (John 9:28-29) This was the way people looked at Jesus. Many who diligently obeyed the letter of the Mosaic Law disobeyed Jesus Christ. The most devout of the religious leaders were the first ones to be judged by Jesus' words and resurrection.

Now at this time I would like to clarify the meaning of "judgement by fire." We read in the New Testament: "...the heavens will be kindled and dissolved, and the elements will melt with fire!" (II Peter 3:12) How can this fantastic prophecy come true? Will it happen literally? No. The statement has symbolic meaning. God would not destroy His earth, His stars and all creation without realizing His ideal on earth. If He did so, then God would become the

God of defeat. And who would be His conqueror? It would be Satan. This can never happen to God.

Even on our human level, once we determine to do something, we see it through to its completion. How much more so will God almighty accomplish His will. When God speaks of judgement by fire in the Bible, He does not mean he will bring judgement by literal flames. The significant meaning is a symbolic one.

Let us now consider another Biblical passage which speaks of fire. Jesus proclaimed, "I came to cast fire upon the earth; and would that it were already kindled!" (Luke 12:49) Did Jesus throw literal, blazing fire about? Of course not.

The fire in the Bible is symbolic. It stands for the word of God. This is why James 3:6 states, "...the tongue is a fire..." The tongue speaks the word, and the word is from God. Jesus himself said, "He who rejects me and does not receive my sayings has a judge; the word that I have spoken will be his judge on the last day." (John 12:48)

In contemporary society, the word of the court executes judgement. The word is the law. In this universe, God is in the position of judge. Jesus came as the advocate with authority to oppose Satan, the prosecutor of human beings. Satan accuses us with his words, but these are false charges. Jesus champions the cause of believers, and his standard is the word of truth. God pronounces the sentence: His love is the standard, and love is His word. There is no difference between the earthly court and the heavenly court, in that both conduct their trials by words, not by fire.

So the world will not be burned up by literal fire when it is judged. The Bible states, " . . . the Lord Jesus will slay him [the evil one] with the breath of his mouth . . . " (II Thess. 2:8) The word of God is the breath of his mouth. Jesus came to slay the wicked by the word of God, and ". . . he shall smite the earth with the rod of his mouth, and with the breath of his lips he shall slay the wicked." (Is. 11:4) What then is the "rod of his mouth?" We take this symbol to mean his tongue—through which he speaks the Word of

God.

Let's resolve this point completely. Look to where Jesus was instructing the people: "Truly, truly, I say to you, he who hears my word and believes him who sent me, has eternal life; he does not come into judgement, but has passed from death to life." (John 5:24) We pass from death to life through words of truth. God will not send you the Messiah to burn you up. He will not send you the Messiah to set your houses afire or destroy your society. But if we reject the Word of God spoken by the Lord, we leave no choice open except to be condemned by judgement. Here is the reason why.

In the beginning God created human beings and the universe by His Word—the logos. Man and woman denied the Word of God and fell. Spiritual death has reigned ever since. Through His salvation work, God has been recreating us. We fell by disobedience to God's Word, and we shall be recreated by obedience to the same Word of God. The Word of God is given by the Lord. Accepting the Word brings life out of death. Such death is the hell in which we live. Thus the Word of God is the judge, and it will bring upon you a far more profound effect than the hottest flames.

6

Jesus And The Second Coming

I am going to speak about some new revelations from God which are very vital to the understanding of all Christians. I will also frequently mention the chosen people of Israel. I am sure there are many Christians and Jewish people in the audience. I dearly love all Christian brothers and sisters, and I have high esteem for the Jewish people. I beg you to understand before I begin that what I will say in no way reflects my personal feeling. I am only bearing witness to the truth.

Sometimes testimony to the truth is a painful task. Yet it is a mission it is my duty to fulfill. The content of my message tonight may be contrary to your previous understanding. Some things may be very new to you. Sometimes it seems as if in the providence, God enjoys seeing people clash. Jesus was a messenger of God who criticized people for being blasphemers and being like serpents and he certainly made some people angry. If Jesus had told the people of his time that they were wonderful children of God, would he have been killed? Without exception the other saints like Confucius and Mohammed also declared to the world something it didn't want to hear. May I ask you to think over seriously what you hear.

What would have happened if the nation of Israel had wholeheartedly accepted Jesus Christ? Imagine the nation of Israel united with Jesus. What would that have meant? First of all, Jesus would not have been killed. People would have glorified Jesus as the living Lord. They would have then gone forward to Rome with the living Christ, and Rome could have received the Son of God in his own lifetime. But in the sad reality of history, it took four centuries for Jesus' disciples to win Rome. Jesus never won the chosen people of Israel, and he never gained the support he needed from them. He came to erect the Kingdom of God on earth, but instead he had to caution his disciples even to keep his identity a secret because people did not accept his legitimacy as the Messiah, and he therefore lacked the power to be the King of kings.

Today we have much to learn, and we must not believe blindly. We must know the hidden truth behind the Bible. Jesus was crucified, not by his own will, but by the will of others. Jesus Christ was killed because humankind would not have faith in him as Messiah.

I am making a bold declaration. Jesus did not come to die. Jesus Christ was murdered. Leaders of the most prepared religion delivered him to be crucified. The Roman governor Pilate wanted to release Jesus, but he was forced to release Barabbas instead. What a pity! What a tragedy!

This may be shocking and astounding news to you, but if you are only surprised, then you have missed my purpose. People living at the time of Jesus Christ made a terrible mistake. But do you think they were so much more ignorant and less aware than we are today? No, not at all. They learned the Old Testament word for word and memorized the Mosaic Law. Based on their understanding, Jesus did not meet the qualifications to be the Messiah.

The nation of Israel at that point was in a very difficult position. If they wanted to fulfill the Law and the Prophets, they had to abandon the Law of Moses as they understood it. Two thousand years of tradition had been based on the Old Testament. It was very, very difficult for people just to wake up one morning, completely revise their interpretation of the Law, and totally accept Jesus Christ as the Son of God. Those leaders who had their eyes riveted to the letter of the Law simply missed the spirit of the Law.

Let us look into the Old Testament and examine the prophecy of Malachi: ". . . I will send you Elijah the prophet before the great and terrible day of the Lord comes. And he will turn the hearts of fathers to their children and the hearts of children to their fathers. . . " (Mal. 4:5-6) The people of Israel knew God's promise clearly. They knew it by heart. And they expected the coming of Elijah before the Messiah appeared. When the Messiah did come, naturally they asked, "Where is Elijah?"

Elijah had been a prophet who performed miraculous works about 900 years before Christ. And it was written he ascended into heaven in a chariot of fire. Since Elijah ascended into heaven, he was expected to return from heaven. Did such a miracle happen before the coming of Jesus? Did the people hear any news about the arrival of Elijah? No, they did not. But what they did hear one day was the voice of Jesus Christ declaring that he was the only begotten "Son of God." And Jesus spoke not timidly, but with authority and power. Such a man could not be ignored.

This presented a great dilemma for the people. They immediately asked, "If this Jesus is the Messiah, then where is Elijah?" They earnestly expected the Messiah at that time, so they were also waiting for Elijah. They believed he would come straight down from heaven, right out of the sky, and the Messiah would come soon after, in a similar manner.

So when Jesus proclaimed himself as the Son of God, the people who heard him became puzzled. If there had come no Elijah, then there could be no Messiah. And no one had told them that Elijah had come. Jesus' disciples were also confused. When they went out to preach the gospel, people persistently denied that Jesus could be the Son of God because the disciples were unable to prove that Elijah had come. They confronted this problem everywhere they went.

The disciples of Jesus were not educated in the Old Testament. Many learned people rebuked them when they went out to preach, asking, "Do you not know the Old Testament? Do you not know the Mosaic Law?" The disciples were embarrassed when they were attacked through the verses of the Law and the prophets. One day they came back to Jesus and put the question to him:

> ". . . why do the scribes say that first Elijah must come?" He replied, "Elijah does come, and he is to restore all things; but I tell you that Elijah has already come, and they did not know him, but did to him whatever they pleased. So also the Son of man will suffer at their hands." Then the disciples understood that he was speaking to them of John the Baptist. (Matt. 17:10-13)

According to Jesus, John the Baptist was Elijah.

This was the truth. We have determined the truth according to the words of Jesus Christ. But the disciples of Jesus could not convince the elders and chief priests and scribes of this fact. The only authority that supported such a notion was the word of Jesus of Nazareth. That is why the testimony of John the Baptist was so crucial. But alas, John himself denied that he was Elijah when he was asked! His denial made Jesus seem to be a liar.

Read the Bible:

> And this is the testimony of John, when the Jews sent priests and Levites from Jerusalem to ask him, "Who are you?" . . . And they asked him, "What then? Are you Elijah?" He said, "I am

not." "Are you the prophet?" And he answered, "No." (John 1:19-21)

John himself said, "I am not Elijah." But Jesus had said, "He is Elijah."

John made it almost impossible for the people to know that Elijah had come. But Jesus declared the truth anyway. He said, ". . . if you are willing to accept it, he [John the Baptist] is Elijah who is to come." (Matt. 11:14) Jesus knew that most people could not accept the truth. Instead they questioned the motivation of Jesus. In order for Jesus to seem like the Messiah, Elijah had to come first, so the people thought he was lying for the purpose of his own self-aggrandizement. The Son of God became more and more misunderstood by the people.

This was such a grave situation. In those days, the influence of John The Baptist was felt in every corner of Israel. But Jesus Christ was an obscure and ambiguous figure in his society. Who was in a position to take Jesus' words as the truth? This failure of John was the major cause of the crucifixion of Jesus.

John the Baptist had already seen the Spirit of God descending upon the head of Jesus Christ at the Jordan River. At that time he testified:

> "I saw the Spirit descend as a dove from heaven, and it remained on him. I myself did not know him; but he who sent me to baptize with water said to me, 'He on whom you see the Spirit descend and remain, this is he who baptizes with the Holy Spirit.' And I have seen and have borne witness that this is the Son of God." (John 1:32-34)

Yes, John the Baptist bore witness, and he did the job that God intended for him to do at that time. But later on, doubts came to him, and he finally succumbed to the many rumors circulating about Jesus. One such rumor called Jesus fatherless, an illegitimate child. John the Baptist certainly heard that rumor, and he wondered how such a person could be the Son of God. Even though he had witnessed to Jesus, John later became suspicious and turned away from him. If John the Baptist had truly united with Jesus Christ, he could have moved his people to accept Jesus as the Messiah, for the power and influence of John was very great in those days.

I am telling you many unusual things, and you may ask by what authority I am speaking. It is the authority of the Bible, with the authority of revelation. Let us read the Bible together, and see word by word how John the Baptist acted.

> Now when John heard in prison about the deeds of the Christ, he sent word by his disciples and said to him, "Are you he who is to come, or shall we look for another?" (Matt. 11:2-3)

This was long after he had testified to Jesus as the Son of God. How could he ask, "Are you he who is to come as the Son of God?" after the testimony of the Spriit to him? Jesus was truly sorrowful. He felt anger. Jesus refused to answer John the Baptist with a straight yes or no. He replied instead, "Blessed is he who take no offense at me." Let me paraphrase what Jesus meant: "John, I am sorry that you took offense at me. At one time you recognized me, but now you doubt me. I am sorry your faith has proved to be so weak."

After this incident, Jesus spoke to the crowds concerning John. He put a rhetorical question to them:

> "What did you go out into the wilderness to behold? A reed shaken by the wind? Why then did you go out? To see a man clothed in soft raiment? Behold, those who wear soft raiment are in kings' houses. Why then did you go out? To see a prophet? Yes, I tell you, and more than a prophet. This is he of whom it is written, 'Behold, I send my messenger before thy face, who shall prepare thy way before thee.' " (Matt. 11:7-10)

Here Jesus affirmed that John was Elijah, the one called by God to turn the people to the Messiah. He praised John from this perspective, concluding with the words, "Truly, I say to you, among those born of women there has risen no one greater than John the Baptist; yet he who is the least in the kingdom of heaven is greater than he." (Matt. 11:11) Conventional Christian interpretations have never fully explained the meaning of this verse.

The missions of the prophets through the ages were to prepare for or testify to the Messiah. Prophets had always testifed from a distance of time. John the Baptist was the greatest among prophets because only he was the prophet contemporary with the Messiah, the prophet who could bear witness, in person, to the living Christ. But John failed to recognize the Messiah. Even the least of the prophets then living in the heavens knew Jesus was the Son of God. That is why John, who was given the greatest mission, and failed, became less than the least.

Thus, Jesus was saying, "John, you went out to the wilderness to serve as the greatest of prophets—you went to find the Messiah, the Son of God. You have seen everything but missed the vital point, the core of your mission. You indeed failed to recognize me and failed to live up to God's expectation. It is God who expects of you 'to make ready for the Lord a people prepared.' You have failed."

Jesus said, "From the days of John the Baptist until now the kingdom of heaven has suffered violence, and men of violence take it by force." (Matt. 11:12) John the Baptist was the chosen instrument of God, destined to be the chief disciple of Jesus, not by "force," but by providence. He failed in his responsibility, and Simon Peter, by the strength and force of his faith, earned that central position for himself. Other men stronger and more violent in faith than John the Baptist fought relentlessly on the side of Jesus for the realization of God's Kingdom on earth. The devout men who righteously followed John the Baptist did not become the twelve apostles and seventy disciples of Christ, as they were to have been. If John the Baptist had become the chief disciple of Jesus, those two together would have united all of Israel. But the truth is that John the Baptist did not follow the Son of God.

One day John's followers came to him and asked, "Rabbi, he who was with you beyond the Jordan, to whom you bore witness, here he is, baptizing, and all are going to him." (John 3:26) They carried concern in their question: "Look at all the people going to Jesus. What about you?" John the Baptist replied, "He must increase, but I must decrease." (John 3:30)

Usually Christians interpret this message as a proof of John's humble personality. This is an incorrect understanding of the significance of his words. If Jesus and John had been united, their destiny would have been to rise or fall together. Then Jesus could not increase his reputation while John's own prestige diminished! The lessening of his own role was what John feared. John once stated that the Messiah was the one ". . . whose sandals I am not worthy to carry; . . ." (Matt. 3:11) Yet he failed to follow Jesus even after he knew that Jesus was the Son of God. John the Baptist was a man without excuse. He should have followed Jesus.

God sent John as a forerunner to the Messiah. His mission was clearly defined, ". . . to make ready for the Lord a people prepared." (Luke 1:17) But because of John's failure, Jesus Christ had no ground upon which to start his ministry. The people had not been prepared to receive Jesus. Therefore, Jesus had to go out from his home and work all by himself, trying to create a foundation on which the people could believe in him. There can be no doubt that John the Baptist was a man of failure. He was directly responsible for the crucifixion of Jesus Christ.

You may again want to ask me, "With what authority do you say these things?" I spoke with Jesus Christ in the spirit world. And I spoke also with John the Baptist. This is my authority. If you cannot at this time determine that my words are the truth, you will surely discover that they are in the course of time. These are hidden truths presented to you as new revelations. You have heard me speak from the Bible. If you believe the Bible you must believe what I am saying.

We must therefore come to this solemn conclusion: The crucifixion of Jesus was a result of human faithlessness. The most egregious and destructive lack of faith was to be found in John. This means that Jesus did not come to die on the cross. If Jesus had come to die, then he would not have offered that tragic and anguished prayer in the garden of Gethsemane. Jesus said to his disciples:

> "My soul is very sorrowful, even to death; remain here, and watch with me." And going a little farther he fell on his face and prayed, "My Father, if it be possible, let this cup pass from me; nevertheless, not as I will, but as thou wilt." (Matt. 26:38-39)

Jesus prayed this way not just once, but three times. If death on the cross had been fulfillment of God's will, Jesus would certainly have prayed instead, "Father, I am honored to die on the cross for your will."

But Jesus prayed asking that this cup pass from him. If his prayer came out of his fear of death, such weakness would disqualify him as the Son of God. We know of the courageous deaths of many martyrs throughout Christian history and even elsewhere, people who not only overcame their fear of death, but made their final sacrifice a great victory. Out of so many martyrs, how could Jesus alone be the one to show his fear and weakness, particularly if his crucifixion was the glorious moment of his fulfillment of the will of God? Jesus did not pray this way from weakness. To believe such a thing is an outrage to Jesus Christ.

The prayer of Jesus at the garden of Gethsemane did not come from his fear of death or suffering. Jesus would have been willing and ready to die a thousand times over if that could have achieved the will of God. He agonized with God together in the garden, and he made one final plea to God, because he knew his death would only cause the prolongation of the dispensation.

Jesus wanted to live and fulfill his primary mission. It is a tragic misunderstanding to believe that Jesus prayed for a little more earthly life out of the frailty of his human soul. Young Nathan Hale, in the American struggle for independence, was able to say at the time of his execution, "I regret that I have but one life to give for my country!" Do you think Jesus Christ was a lesser soul than Nathan Hale? No! Nathan Hale was a great patriot. But Jesus Christ is the Son of God.

Think this over. If Jesus came to die on the cross, would he not need a man to deliver him up? You know that Judas Iscariot is the disciple who betrayed Jesus. If Jesus fulfilled God's will with his death on the cross, then Judas should be glorified as the man who made the crucifixion possible. Judas would have been aiding God's dispensation. But Jesus said of Judas, "The Son of man goes as it is written of him, but woe to that man by whom the Son of man is betrayed! It would have been better for that man if he had not been born." (Matt. 26:24) Judas killed himself.

Furthermore, if God had wanted His son to be crucified, He did not need 4,000 years to prepare the chosen people. He would have done better to send Jesus to a savage tribe, where he could have been killed even faster, and the will of God would have been realized more rapidly.

I must tell you again, it was the will of God to have Jesus Christ accepted by his people. That is why God labored in hope and anguish to prepare fertile soil for the heavenly seed of the Messiah. That is why God established His chosen people of Israel. That is why God sent prophet after prophet to awaken the people of Israel to ready themselves for the Lord.

God warned them and chastised them; He persuaded them and scolded them, pushed them and punished them because He wanted His people to accept His Son. One day Jesus was asked, " 'What must we do, to be doing the works of God?' Jesus answered them, 'This is the work of God,

that you believe in him whom he has sent.' " (John 6:28-29)
Israel did the very thing God had labored to prevent. She
rejected the one He had sent.

Jesus had one purpose throughout the three years of his
public ministry: Acceptance. He could not fulfill his mission
otherwise. From the very first day, he preached the gospel
without equivocation, so that the people could hear the
truth and accept him as the Son of God. The word of God
should have led them to accept him. However, when Jesus
saw that the people were not likely to receive him by the
words of God alone, he began to perform mighty works. He
hoped that people could recognize him through his mira-
cles.

> Now Jesus did many other signs in the presence
> of the disciples, which are not written in this
> book; but these are written that you may believe
> that Jesus is the Christ, the Son of God, and that
> believing you may have life in his name. (John
> 20:30-31)

Jesus gave sight to the blind and made the lepers clean.
He healed the lame and blessed the deaf with hearing. Jesus
raised the dead. He did these things only because he wanted
to be accepted. Yet the people said of him, "It is only by
Beelzebul, the prince of demons, that this man casts out
demons." (Matt. 12:24) What a heartbreaking situation!
Jesus soon saw the hopelessness of gaining the acceptance of
the people. In anger and desperation he chastised them:
"You brood of vipers! . . ." (Matt. 12:34) He did not hide
his wrath, but exploded in anger. "Woe to you, Chorazin!
woe to you, Bethsaida! for if the mighty works done in you
had been done in Tyre and Sidon, they would have repented
long ago in sackcloth and ashes." (Matt. 11:21) And he wept
when he drew near the city of Jerusalem.

> "O Jerusalem, Jerusalem, killing the prophets
> and stoning those who are sent to you! How
> often would I have gathered your children

> together as a hen gathers her brood under her
> wings, and you would not!" (Matt. 23:37)

Who has ever understood the broken heart of Jesus? He said, "Would that even today you knew the things that make for peace! But now they are hid from your eyes." (Luke 19:42) By that time Jesus knew there was absolutely no hope of avoiding death. Yet he pleaded with God in Gethsemane, and he pleaded with God on the cross: "My God, my God, why hast thou forsaken me?" (Matt. 27:46)

Thus Jesus died on the cross, not to fulfill his own ultimate hope, not because of God's original plan, but by the will of sinful people. Christ was destined to return from that moment on. He will return to consummate his mission on earth. Mankind must await his second coming for the complete salvation of the world.

Many people may now ask, "What about the prophecies in the Old Testament concerning the death of Jesus on the cross?" I am aware of those prophecies, such as Isaiah, Chapter 53. We must know that there are dual lines of prophecy in the Bible. One group prophesies Jesus' rejection and death; the others, such as Isaiah, Chapters 9, 11, and 60, prophesy the glorious ministry of Jesus when the people accepted him as the Son of God, as the King of kings. For example:

> For to us a child is born, to us a son is given; and
> the government will be upon his shoulder, and
> his name will be called "Wonderful Counselor,
> Mighty God, Everlasting Father, Prince of
> Peace." Of the increase of his government and of
> peace there will be no end, upon the throne of
> David, and over his kingdom, to establish it, and
> to uphold it with justice and with righteousness
> from this time forth and forevermore . . . (Is.
> 9:6-7)

This is the prophecy of the Lord of glory, Jesus as the King of kings, and Prince of Peace. On the other hand, we can read:

> Surely he has borne our griefs and carried our
> sorrows; yet we esteemed him stricken, smitten
> by God, afflicted. But he was wounded for our
> transgressions, he was bruised for our iniquities;
> upon him was the chastisement that made us
> whole, and with his stripes we are healed. (Is.
> 53:4-5)

This is the prophecy of the suffering Christ. It is indeed the prophecy of the crucifixion.

Then why did God prophesy in two contradictory ways in the Bible? It is because God has to deal with us—fallen human beings—in His dispensation. And fallen people are wicked and untrustworthy and possess the capacity of betrayal.

In a way God fears us, and Satan fears us also—because of our ability to betray. God is absolute good, and He never changes His position; Satan is absolute evil, and he never changes his position either. In this respect God and Satan are similar. However, we are a mixture of good and evil. We stand between God and Satan and have the ability to change. Therefore, we are unpredictable. One day a person may profess untiring faith in God and desire to serve Him; and the next day the same person may curse God, unite with Satan and become his slave.

Since God did not know how the people would respond to His providence for the Messiah, He had no choice but to predict two contradictory results—dual prophecies, each possibility depending on human actions. Thus the people's faith was the factor determining which one of the two prophecies would be fulfilled.

In the case of Jesus, if people demonstrated faith by uniting with him, then he would be accepted. The full realization of the prophecy of the Lord of glory would result.

On the other hand, if people lacked faith in him and rejected the Messiah when he came, inevitably the second prophecy, that of the suffering Christ, would be fulfilled.

And history shows that there was insufficient faith in Jesus when he came. Therefore, the prophecy of the suffering Lord became reality instead of the prophecy of the Lord of glory. Thus the crucifixion and the story of the suffering Christ became the course of history.

In the Old Testament religion, the priest had the qualification to kill the offering, put it on the altar, and ask God to accept the offering. There must be someone who cuts the offering into two and puts it on the altar; then it can be accepted by God. The priest of all priests was Jesus Christ. He was supposed to put the whole nation of Israel, the chosen nation, in the position of the sacrifice. He has to sacrifice the whole nation; and the nation should not have complained, being in the position of the offering. But they did, and their disbelief in him led Jesus to die in their place as the offering. God is not a person who wants to see bloodshed. But in order to save fallen humanity, God had to do that. Because Jesus as a human being shed his blood, God had a reasonable condition to restore humanity. That's why He was forced to send Jesus to the cross.

The Bible does not provide much record of the life of Jesus prior to his public ministry, except for the story of his birth and a few accounts of his childhood. Haven't you ever wondered why?

For thirty years Jesus lived in great rejection and humiliation. There were many events and circumstances which grieved and agonized Jesus. He was truly a misunderstood person—in his society and even among his own family. Nobody, absolutely nobody treated him as the Son of God. He was not even accorded the common respect due to any man. His society ridiculed him. God's heart was very deeply grieved by Jesus' life. If I revealed just a glimpse of some of the situations of heartbreak and sorrow in the life of Jesus, that obscure figure, the man of Nazareth, you would not only be shocked and stunned, but you would burst into tears of sorrow.

God did not wish humankind to know the tragedy, the heart-breaking reality of the humiliation of Jesus Christ.

The death of Jesus was neither his will not his fault. The death of Jesus was murder. Our salvation in Christianity comes not from the cross but from the resurrection. Without the resurrection, Christianity has no power. The resurrected Jesus brought new hope, new forgiveness, and a new power of salvation. Therefore, when we place our faith in the Jesus Christ of resurrection and unite with him, our salvation comes.

Jesus' greatest declaration was that he was the only begotten Son of God. What is a begotten son? He is the trunkline, the only object or recipient of the full love of God. Jesus proclaimed that he came in the position of bridegroom to all humanity, but he also placed himself on the horizontal level, relating to everyone as a neighbor, teacher, brother and friend. When you read the Bible, it is obvious that Jesus is the trunkline of God's truth and love.

Jesus knew the heart of God, and when he was crucified he said, "Oh my God, my God, why hast thou forsaken me?" The crucifixion brought tremendous grief to the heart of God; God had sent him down as His only begotten son, and God deeply wanted to see Jesus as the center of His only begotten family, only begotten society, national and world. That was God's hope. When that hope was crushed by the rebellion and faithlessness of the people, it became God's desire to send another Messiah, a second son here on earth. Once God conceives His will can He give it up simply because of the situation on earth?

Jesus could not give up the will of God by resenting the adamant opposition to him. Jesus certainly could not abandon his mission at that moment by hating the people. He was a true man because he perfectly lived the life of God. He was a walking God, the fruit of the truth—of God's Logos. There was no separation between God and Jesus, and because no one can destroy God no one can destroy Jesus Christ. The crucifixion was not his destruction; God manifested the power of resurrection so that the world could see that Jesus was never destroyed.

Christianity has spiritual parents. Jesus is in the spiritual father's position, and the Holy Spirit is in the spiritual mother's position. We are given rebirth by following a spiritual father and spiritual mother, but we can only receive spiritual salvation. Therefore, the Christian tradition has been denying the physical world. With Jesus Christ and the Holy Spirit working together we cleanse our sins and are given rebirth on the spiritual level. After the crucifixion of Jesus the Christian foundation could only be a spiritual one, although initially God intended a physical foundation as well.

Today many Christians put exclusive emphasis upon salvation by the blood of Jesus. How mistaken that is in the sight of God! In the Bible is recorded the story of a prostitute who was condemned to death and about to be stoned. Jesus said to the people gathered around her, "Whoever is without sin, let him cast the first stone." Everyone self-consciously dropped their stones. After everyone had drifted away in shame, Jesus spoke to the accused woman, saying, "Has no one condemned you? Neither do I condemn you. Go and sin no more."

What does this mean? By his own words Jesus offered forgiveness. Even before Jesus shed one drop of blood there was already forgiveness from sin. No one had to wait for Jesus to die. There was this path to salvation in accepting the world of Jesus even at that time. That's in the Bible. He did not give a raincheck by saying, "I will forgive you and save you, but wait until I die on the cross." Jesus could open the way to salvation to everyone by the Word of God. God's plan of salvation does not require bloodshed by necessity. Salvation means that the garden of Eden shall be here on earth, with living men, women and families. What we need is living consummation, realizing the love Jesus brought, not alienation, bloodshed and death.

Many Christians today truly misunderstand. They preach resurrection, but resurrection does not mean that dead bodies will rise again. That's a misconception. Death came when human beings departed from God, through the misuse of the love of God. Human physical bodies remained alive after the fall. Resurrection means accepting the word of God to become the possessor of God's love. Suppose Jesus appeared here. Would you want to have only the spiritual salvation which came through the shedding of blood, or would you want to have the living, working salvation of soul and body? Would you want spirit and body restored together by the living Jesus?

Then to what degree should we be like Jesus? You have to reach the point where you are one with Jesus in flesh and blood. That's why he set up the condition of the sacrament: Christians must feel they are actually eating Jesus' flesh and blood. They should actually feel Jesus' life and love more than anything else when eating the bread; and when drinking the wine they should really feel they are drinking his blood. Without such feeling salvation cannot begin at that moment. This was Jesus' method to bring humankind to pass from Satan's world into God's, thus uniting himself with the believer through actual, real sense experience. It means Satan is cut off and humanity is engrafted to Jesus—a consummation with him resulting in one flesh, one blood, i.e. one humanness. Then we can feel this oneness. From that point on the person receives God's love and life. But Christianity further envisions people going through total salvation, both on the physical and spiritual levels. With Christianity as it now stands, we cannot be saved on both levels. That's why Jesus has to come again; and only around the mission of the Second Advent can we gain physical salvation, fulfilling the prophecy of the Lord of Glory. Since the prophecy of the suffering Christ became fact in the time of Jesus, the prophecy of the Lord of glory has been left unfulfilled. And this is the prophecy which will be fulfilled at the time of the Lord of the Second Advent.

Please ask seriously in your prayers guidance on these matters. Ask either Jesus Christ or God himself. If Jesus had lived and fulfilled his primary mission of bringing the Kingdom of God on earth, Christianity would never have been what it is today. The purpose of Jesus' coming was for the salvation of the world. The chosen people were to be God's instruments. However, salvation was not intended only for God's chosen people. For every soul upon the face of the earth, Jesus is the savior. He is the savior of all humankind. Since Jesus left this world prematurely, he also left us the promise of his second coming.

The Christians are the second Israelites, but the Messiah has not arrived yet. In the Christian world, there is no such thing as a national foundation because there is no nation of God's choice on the physical level. If you compare the first Israelites to the second Israelites, the Christian world, which is of more value? The nation of the first Israelites, though small in territory, had sovereignity on both the physical and spiritual levels, and it was in that sense greater than the second Israelite nation, which on the spiritual level has covered almost the whold world, but has not been able to set up anything like a true nation on the physical level.

Should the Messiah come to the Christian world alone, or to the whole world? What God, together with the Christians, must do is cover the whole world both on the spiritual and physical levels. In light of those things, do you think the Messiah should come in the flesh or just in spirit?

In the ideal world we are going to build, we will be liberated from sin both on the physical and spiritual levels, under the actual guidance of God as our parent. The Lord must come again in the flesh to accomplish his mission of saving the physical world. If he comes on the clouds of Heaven, spiritually, he cannot accomplish his mission of restoring the whole world both on the spiritual and physical levels. The problem is the sin and corruption of this world, and not of heaven.

How will the Lord come at the second advent? Our position as Christians exactly parallels the position of the elders, scribes and priests at the time of Jesus. In those days, the people were waiting for Elijah and the Messiah to arrive on the clouds of heaven. Why did the people think this way? Why did they hold this kind of belief?

They were simply following the Bible prophecy written

down in Daniel 7:13: "I saw in the night visions, and behold, with the clouds of heaven there came one like a son of man, and he came to the Ancient of Days and was presented before him." Because of the great prophet Daniel, the people of Israel had every reason to expect the arrival of the Messiah with the clouds of heaven. Christians are expecting the arrival of the Lord in the same way today, from the clouds of heaven.

John said, ". . . many deceivers have gone out into the world, men who will not acknowledge the coming of Jesus Christ in the flesh; such a one is the deceiver and the antichrist." (II John 7) The Bible says that many people were denying the appearance of Jesus Christ in the flesh. And John condemned those people as the antichrist. But let us not forget the Old Testament prophecy of the coming of the Son of God in the clouds of heaven. Unless we know the whole truth, we, like the people of Jesus's time, become victims of the words of the Bible.

The people 2,000 years ago expected the Lord's arrival on the clouds of heaven; so when Jesus appeared in the flesh it was very difficult to accept him. So at that time, there were arguments among Jesus' disciples and the faithful of Israel. "Well, if your master, Jesus, is the Son of God, how could he appear as a man, in the flesh—impossible! How could he be the Son of God? We know him; he is the son of Joseph, the son of Mary. How could he be the son of God? The son of God must come on the clouds of heaven."

So how could they accept Jesus? On what grounds? Those who believed the letter of the Old Testament, and not the spirit, could miss the whole thing. Then how will the Lord appear in the last days? We are in a situation exactly parallel to that of the time of Jesus Christ. If we become slaves to the letter of the New Testament, instead of free in the *spirit* of the New Testament, we will commit the same crime which the elders, scribes, and pharisees committed 2,000 years ago.

Then, may I ask, what would you do if the Lord returned to earth not in the clouds but as a man in the flesh? What would you do? I am telling you, the Lord at the second advent will in fact appear as a Son of man with flesh and bones. The first thing you may want to say is, "Rev. Moon, you are a heretic." But listen for a moment.

It is important to know on which side God will be and how God fulfills His plan. It is not important whether a man or his views are considered heretical or not. It does not matter how I look at the world or how you look at the world. It only matters how God looks at the world. And in God's view, we once again find in the Bible a dual prophecy concerning the coming of the Lord of the Second Advent. Revelation 1:7 definitely prophesies the arrival of the Lord with the clouds. However, I Thess. 5:2 states: "For you yourselves know well that the day of the Lord will come like a thief in the night." There are then two opposing prophecies. What shall we do? Would you simply choose the prophecy which is most convenient for you?

Perhaps the Lord will appear with a loud noise in the clouds of heaven, because the prophecy says so. But on the other hand, the Lord may appear like a thief in the night. If he comes on the clouds, he surely cannot slip into the world unseen like a thief. Tremendous attention would surround the spectacle of his coming on the clouds. I cannot imagine how such a thing could be hidden from your eyes.

Then just what is the truth? We have a crucial question before us. What is the truth? When you see the signs of the Last Days, the Bible urges you to go into a dark room and pray. Who can tell you the time of the Last Days? The angels do not know that day. Jesus said not even the Son of man knew when that day would arrive. Only God knows the time of the Last Days. That is why we have our answer from God. I am not saying you must believe me—not at all. I am just revealing what I know to be the truth, but you must verify this truth with God.

Most Christians today do not know the position they have. They simply believe in Jesus Christ and accept the words of the Bible. They feel that some day Jesus will come on the clouds of heaven, and all true Christians will be lifted up in the air. Somehow they will have a rendezvous with Jesus and have some kind of millennium up there. That is horrendous, empty, hollow. Religion is not out there, up in the stratosphere.

I am testifying that the Lord cannot appear in that kind of supernatural fashion. Jesus Christ could not return that way because the work of God is to be done here on earth. The mission of the Messiah is a physical, realistic one. As a man he must come up from the bottom of human misery. He must come to the most miserable nation and lift the human status from the slave position, to the servant position, to the adopted child position and to the direct child position by physically putting together the Kingdom of Heaven here on earth. That is the mission of the Messiah.

In the Last Days, the Bible says, do not just believe anybody. Do not believe me, and do not believe someone just because of his or her official status in church or society. Famous leaders will not necessarily give you the guidance God would want for you. Heaven is so near, and you can be lifted up by the spirit so high, that you can speak with God and receive the answer directly from Him if you are earnest enough.

There are many ministers in America, many clergymen and many church elders. How many of them are really listening for the voice of God? These ears of ours do not mean much, nor these eyes serve any useful purpose, unless we have sprritual ears and spiritual eyes. Jesus said, "He who has ears to hear, let him hear." (Matt. 11:15) And he said to his disciples, "But blessed are your eyes, for they see, and your ears, for they hear." (Matt. 13:16) He was not referring to physical sense organs.

When you use your spiritual senses and listen for the Word of God, you will find His direction and guidance. But it is not easy to become a citizen of the Kingdom of Heaven. It is very difficult for a foreigner just to become a citizen of the United States. How much more difficult it is to remove ourselves from our corrupt life and transfer ourselves into the Kingdom of Heaven. But we can achieve this very thing.

We know that even after Adam and Eve fell in the garden of Eden, they still were able to communicate directly with God. Do you think that since the says of the Old and New Testaments, God has for some reason become deaf and dumb? No, God is very much alive, and today we can talk directly to Him. God can speak to you, and you can have a direct confrontation with Him. The Acts of the Apostles says that in the last days, ". . . your sons and your daughters shall prophesy and your young men shall see visions, and your old men shall dream dreams; . . ." (Acts 2:17) We must know the truth. We have to know how to apply for citizenship into the Kingdom of God. We have to know when the Lord will come, and how he will arrive.

Let us look to our Bible and clarify how the Lord of the Second Advent will appear. In Luke 17:20-21, the Pharisees asked Jesus how the Kingdom of God was coming. He answered, "The Kingdom of God is not coming with signs to be observed; . . . the Kingdom of God is in the midst of you." Jesus then told his disciples, "The days are coming when you will desire to see one of the days of the Son of man, and you will not see it." But if the Lord comes in the clouds of heaven, how could we not see it? Yet Revelation 1:7 says. ". . . every eye will see him, every one who pierced him; . . ." What can this mean? Why would we not see him? The only way we might miss that day is if we look for the Lord to come from one direction, and he appears from another direction in an entirely unexpected manner, just as Elijah did at the time of Jesus. This is the reason you may not see the Lord at the time of his second coming.

Another mysterious prediction was given by Jesus Christ himself. He declared about the Lord at the second coming: "But first he must suffer many things and be rejected by this generation." (Luke 17:25) If Christ at his Second Coming appears in the glory of the clouds of heaven, who would deny him? Nobody would cause him suffering and pain. The only way this prophecy can be fulfilled is if people expect his return from the clouds and he suddenly appears as a humble man in the flesh. Do you think that Christian leaders of today would make the same mistake that the priests and scribes and elders committed at the time of Jesus? Yes! They may very well deny him and reject him, because the manner of his coming would be very difficult for Christian leaders to accept. However, in this way the Bible will be fulfilled. He will first suffer and be rejected by this generation.

Jesus once asked a most important question: "When the Son of man comes, will he find faith on earth?" (Luke 18:8) How does this question concern us today, when Christian faith covers the face of the earth? It is because although we do have faith today, it may be mistaken faith—a belief which expects the Lord must come on the clouds of heaven. There are few men or women on earth with the kind of faith ready to accept the Son of Man appearing in the flesh. If this were not the situation, the Bible prophecy we are discussing here would not be fulfilled. Please note that Jesus did not say there would be no believers, but he said there would be no faith.

Jesus also said.

> "Not every one who says to me, 'Lord, Lord,' shall enter the kingdom of heaven, but he who does the will of my Father who is in heaven. On that day many will say to me, 'Lord, Lord, did we not prophesy in your name, and cast out demons in your name, and do many mighty works in your name? And then will I declare to them. 'I never knew you; depart from me, you evil-doers.' " (Matt. 7:21-23)

This prophecy cannot be realized if his second coming is on the clouds of heaven.

At the time of the second advent, people again will be crying out, "Lord, Lord." At the same time they may be in the process of trying to crucify the Messiah if he appears in a manner different from their expectations. They will then be the worst evildoers.

This is the Bible. Those who truly have eyes will see. Those who truly have ears will hear. Throughout history, God has sent His prophets before the time of fulfillment. He warns the people of His plan. No matter how devout Christian faith is today, no matter how many millions of people are in the Christian churches, they and their churches and their world will decline once they fail to accept the Lord, however he may appear. This was the tragic fate of Israel and the Roman Empire when they denied Jesus Christ, regardless of their righteousness otherwise.

We must therefore also be open to a new message. Jesus Christ did not come to repeat the Mosaic Law. Just as Jesus revealed himself with the new expression of truth, the Lord at the second advent will reveal himself with God's truth for our time. That truth will not be simply a repetition of the New Testament.

The first ancestors lost the kingdom of God on earth. Satan invaded the world and took Eve to his side, and then Eve took Adam away, leaving God alone and separated from His children. All humankind has therefore suffered under the bondage of evil. God must therefore send a new ancestor for humanity, to begin a new history. The work of God is restoration, always in the opposite direction from His original loss. This means that God first needs to find His perfected Adam, an Adam who instead of betraying God will become one with God. And then Adam must restore his bride in the position of Eve. Perfected Adam and perfected Eve, united together, will be able to overcome Satan and expel him from the world. In this way, the first righteous ancestors of humankind will begin a new history.

God's first beginning was alpha. This was invaded by evil, so He will restore the world in omega. Jesus is referred to as the last Adam in I Cor. 15:45. God wanted to bless Adam and Eve in marriage when they were perfected. As a heavenly couple, they could bear children of God. This life was not realized in the garden of Eden. That is why Jesus came in the postion of Adam. God intended to find the true bride and have Jesus marry. The True Parents of humankind would have been inaugurated in the time of Jesus, and they could have overcome and changed the evil history of the world. Since that hope was not completed by Jesus, after 2,000 years he is returning to earth as a man to complete in full the mission he only partially accomplished. The Kingdom of Heaven on earth will be established at that time.

Christians are looking for God just in their thoughts, very vaguely, on the spiritual level alone. They cherish the hope of going to live in the spirit world, and glorify it alone, without minding the physical world. Of course, the true Kingdom of God on earth will be both the spiritual and physical levels. When Jesus prayed at Gethsemene, he begged and begged God to let that cup pass from him, because he knew only too well that if he died on the cross, the will of God both on the spiritual and physical levels would be left unaccomplished. In the Old Testament Age, when the Israelites chosen by God were preparing to receive the Messiah they formed a nation both on the spiritual and physical levels. But when Jesus came, he could accomplish his mission only on the spiritual level, so the physical level is left for the Lord to accomplish at the second advent, in order to realize the Kingdom of God on earth both on the spiritual and physical levels.

The question is, who is going to accomplish God's will on the physical level? It is natural that the Lord at the second coming who will come representing Jesus should accomplish that mission, just as Jesus came as the Messiah representing Adam. Jesus was the second Adam, and the Lord at the second advent will be the third Adam. This messiah must work upon the foundation of Jesus Christ, so he's going to do on the physical level what Jesus did on the spiritual level.

The new history of goodness will thus begin. With the truth of God and True Parents for humanity, a new alpha in God's history will begin and continue for eternity. The ideal of God is to restore the first perfect God-centered family on earth. With this one model as a center, all the rest of the world can be adopted into this family. We will become like them, and the first heavenly family will be expanded, multiplying into the tribal, national, and worldwide Kingdom of God on earth.

The Kingdom of Heaven is to be literal and tangible. Jesus gave Peter the keys to the Kingdom and said, ". . . whatever you bind on earth shall be bound in heaven, and whatever you loose on earth shall be loosed in heaven." (Matt. 16:19) So accomplishment on earth must precede fulfillment in heaven; the Kingdom of Heaven will be first achieved on earth. At this time only an intermediate place in the spirit world is open. That is called, "Paradise." Jesus and his disciples dwell in Paradise, and even they cannot actually enter the Kingdom of Heaven until it is established on earth. One reason for this is because the Kingdom of Heaven is prepared not for individuals, but for the family of God— for the father, the mother, and God's true children.

If in the Christian world people cling to the old traditions, can they go with the Messiah to the world of new dimension? Up to the present moment people have been safe in believing in Christ—just in belief, they are settled in belief. But when Jesus Christ appears again they must not only believe in him but follow him. If you receive Jesus Christ, would he want you to just accept him as the Christ and believe in him, or would he want you to know him, understand his heart, and follow him? He would want us to know him and understand him, his heart. And he would even want you to act in place of him, doing what he would have you do. The Lord will not appear miraculously in the clouds of heaven, because God is sending His son to restore the things that were lost on earth. Would humankind prefer to receive a Messiah who came dramatically on a cloud, without teaching and being all those things which Jesus was, or a Messiah who came normally but was able to convey those precious understandings? Certainly, we would value the second kind of Messiah.

Up to now, most people thought of Christianity in terms

of their own group, their own nation, but from now on our scope must become larger than that, encompassing the whole world. The scope of our thought must be broadened so as to get the whole world involved. In the Christian churches we must deal with problems of the world transcending national boundaries in order to receive things of new dimension. We must even create a new dimension of culture. The Lord at the second advent comes for the whole world, for the salvation of the whole world. Then those who follow him must receive his idea and think of things in terms of the world, not of the individual. If Jesus were here, when he saw that a vast number of denominations had been created, would he be glad? Christianity started from his teaching, which was one, not many. Then when they find many Christian denominations in disharmony among themselves, God is not happy over that and Jesus Christ is not happy over that. God did not send Jesus Christ to create so many denominations. Then when Jesus sees that there are so many denominations created after him, he must feel responsibility for that fact. Then if there appears a group of people who will think of the salvation of the whole world and work for that goal, Jesus will be happy about that fact and will come to aid them and God will also come to aid that group. People may not know the particulars and details of the group, but since there is God's will working in it, both God and Jesus will work through the group, in the group.

I believe my message is absolutely clear and simple. God intended to begin the history of goodness in Adam and Eve. But they fell. God worked to restore history and begin anew in Jesus Christ. But the people of his time lacked faith and did not give him a chance. Therefore, Jesus' promise of his return will be fulfilled. The Messiah is destined to come to earth as the Son of Man in the flesh. He comes as the third Adam. He will take a bride and thereby bring about the most joyful day of heavenly matrimony, referred to as "the marriage supper of the Lamb" in the book of Revelation. They will fulfill the role of True Parents. True ancestry from God will be established and heaven on earth can then be literally achieved.

The foundation for the Messiah has to be Christianity because Christianity is the only religion to understand that the true nature of God is that of Father. Jesus was the only man who called himself the only begotten son of God. No other religion is founded upon such a teaching. Jesus was indeed the Messiah because God was his Father and he was His only begotten son. Thus the religion that he founded must become the foundation for the second coming of the Messiah, when God's original love will be fulfilled. Centering upon original love, Christianity creates the godly family of Father, Son, brothers and sisters in Christ—this family concept had to be the mainstream of Gods' dispensation up to the time of the ultimate fulfillment.

Christianity had to become the most widespread religion in the world because God has a big stake in it; He has a plan for fulfilling His dispensation through it. Unfortunately, traditional Christianity was misled by incorrect theology. There are many mistaken ideas, such as Jesus came only to die. Likewise many Christians are content to worry only about their individual salvation, disregarding the matters of this world for their own little heaven. The concept of being saved by faith alone is a very partial view; along with having faith one must fulfill love in order to go to Heaven. Without the power of love, one can never be separated from satanic bondage.

For this reason, God promised humankind that the second Messiah would come as the representative of His original love, bringing liberation from satanic bondage. How can you recognize the second Messiah? The Messiah will teach this principle exactly, point by point, spelling it out. The Bible promises that when the end of the world comes, we will no longer have to be taught by symbols and parables but we will learn plainly of the Father. (John 16:25) That is what the Unification teaching is all about; that is what you are receiving.

At the heart of Christianity is the relationship between the bridegroom and bride. In a spiritual sense, the Christian churches are to prepare themselves with the attitude of a bride. When the Messiah does come in the end times, he will be a living bridegroom to be received by all humanity. Even though we may have understood this concept, we are not living up to our responsibility. Jesus' will and God's will have been very much misrepresented for 2,000 years. The churches have fallen short of the will of God. Therefore, in preparation for the coming of the Messiah, a new Christianity must emerge, and the present churches which have deviated from the will of God must revitalize themselves. That true Christianity must come about. What form must that new Christianity take?

The new Christianity must be the highest form of religion, perfectly fitting the criteria of God's true religion. Christians must fulfill both the wishes of the Messiah and the wishes of God. In order to do so they must elevate themselves to the position of messiah and literally save the world. Their attitude must be: "For the sake of the world I must be a sacrifice. For the sake of God I can sacrifice my Christian church." Centering upon God is absolute obedience, we Christians must bring unity between God and humanity in reality here on earth. As restored Adam and Eve, we must go beyond the level of fulfillment in the garden of Eden; in order to restore their failure, we must make ourselves superior in obedience, in trust, and in love. Therefore we must go beyond the limit of our life.

When Jesus ascended into heaven, he brought down the Holy Spirit, which is the spiritual mother. Eve gave birth to sinful children, but the Holy Spirit comes to give us spiritual rebirth.

Through the power of love a father and mother create new life, and it is the same in the rebirth process. Each person must go back to the origin and be born again, beginning as flesh and blood and bone in the Father. So you must go back to the body of Jesus in a sinless, sacrificial life. If you love Jesus and know that he is your spiritual father, then you must want to bring yourself inside his heart and be born again as his flesh and blood. That's the desire you must have.

Through sacrificial love you can go back to the origin, the very source of your life. Once you were flesh and bone of your father and mother. If you love Jesus so much that nothing else in the world matters to you, you can absolutely give your heart and soul to him. At that point the Holy Spirit can come to you and give you rebirth; they you are reborn as a spiritual son or daughter of Jesus. That is the whole process of rebirth in Christianity. It is the essence of Christianity, but it will elevate a person only to the level of adopted son or daughter.

We are not created in spirit alone, but with a body. The ultimate step left to be taken is to be born again, not just in spirit, but in spirit and body together. For that purpose Jesus' body is needed and he must return as a living person in the flesh. So far Christianity has offered only the possibility of rebirth in spirit. Now in the new age, when Jesus comes back as the second messiah, we shall be given the power to be born again in the body as well. Each person needs this physical rebirth before going to the spirit world. Furthermore, the requirement to enter the Kingdom of God in heaven is that you become elevated as sons and daughters of God, loving the world as God loves the world.

We cannot doubt that Christianity today is in definite crisis. This is a crisis parallel to the time of Jesus, when the established religious institutions failed the Son of God. In the present world tradition has become a shackle, and religions have no way to advance; their former disciplines or traditions are too small to embrace the world. This is why young people are so rebellious in their search for a more open atmosphere. When we see the imbalance and contradiction between the secular world and religious world, we can only conclude that if God is involved at all with this world then the time has come for Him to undertake some extraordinary, revolutionary action to change completely the format of religion.

God must have some universal religion in His mind. Because the world is ready, this is about the time that God will inspire such a religion. Without this religion the present world cannot have any hope for the future. God must have a solution for both the religious and secular worlds together, since He is responsible for them both. Which course shall we take? We have to change either the secular world first or religion first. Certainly religions today must lead the way, through the emergence of a new, universal religion.

The first problem facing this religious revolution is the resolution of religious division and antagonism. Would God want all religious people united together? The universal goal of humankind is world brother and sisterhood—the human family. A new religious movement with that vision and goal should come into being.

Religious people are always a problem to those in power. God is always their goal. Therefore, they can go beyond national boundaries, racial boundaries and cultural boundaries. They are just impossible people to deal with because the accepted sense of judgement does not apply to them. Throughout history, sovereignties have always felt threatened by new religious groups. They are such difficult people to deal with because they cannot be controlled. To say, "We will kill you!" is not a threat to them. They answer, "Go ahead, do it!"

Therefore, as new religions emerged throughout history, governments usually opposed them. They always wanted to liquidate the religions before they got too big. A sovereign nation worries only about the integrity of its own territory, but religious people go beyond the boundary of the nation. Religious people don't care if an enemy is next door. They might even open the door to the enemy camp. This worries the governing people. Rulers of nations usually look at religious people as a very sticky problem.

And yet, today, young people are searching for spiritual values. There is absolutely no other way they can find what they want. Furthermore, the growing interest in religion is reflected in the rising enrollment in church-run schools. This is one indication that the people who could not find secular solutions are coming all the way back to seek out a religious life. Long ago I predicted that this would happen, and that the year 1976 would be a turning point in American history. From now on the search for spiritual rather than material solutions for this nation's problems will intensify. We recognize this crisis in our time; and we can also see through the haze to the brightly shining day of new hope.

We are truly living in an extraordinary time in human history. We are in a position to save and liberate Jesus Christ and end his anguish. We can be in a position to liberate even God. We are the ones who can assure God his happiness, His joy, His peace. We are going to liberate the heart of God and His anguish and sorrow. And by doing so, we are liberating all humankind and its burden and sorrow. Finally, we can push the entire satanic world out of the world.

We are bearing our cross as living beings. In our situation complaining could be possible. But we must go beyond that. We must effect a miracle, such that without dying, we can accomplish this goal—this is the miracle. If you have this faith, this commitment, then when you go, God is with you. His power is yours; God has been with me when I have this intent, this faith, and this love. God was with me each step of my way. The same God shall be with you.

This is the time for unprecedented spiritual awakening. I want you to open your eyes and ears to perceive the truth. This is my hope, that by sharing this message with you, we might unite to prepare for the glorious day of the arrival of the Lord. Let us see the God of history, let us understand the God of Providence, and let us embrace the living God in our own lives.

The major criticism Christians have is their contention that I pose as the Lord of the Second Advent. But I never said that. They created rumors like that. Christians have been waiting all these years for the second coming, so they should have had the courtesy to come and find out for themselves whether our members have valid reason to spread such a rumor. If they had earnestly done that,

Christianity today would be entirely different. Some Christians say that we are heretics, but I tell you that this is not just ordinary heresy. I am a super-heretic in their eyes, and the amazing thing is that God likes this super-heretic.

Children have been born all over the world since Jesus died. Even though they are sinful children, they are still children of God and need to be restored, but there has existed no tree of life for them to physically graft themselves onto. The end of the world is at hand, not only for Christians but for all people throughout the world. The new history of God will begin with the arrival of the Lord. Blessed are those who see him and accept him. It is the hope of Christianity to recognize, receive, and accept the Lord at the second advent. The chance has arrived for all of us. The greatest opportunity in anyone's lifetime is now knocking at our door. Please be humble, and open yourself to great new hope!

No knowledge, no position, no wealth, no anything, nothing can please God except for your heart of love for God alone, which will make Him cry—that alone can touch His heart. If you are ready to do anything at all for Him in order to ease His heart—if you can deny yourself, sacrifice yourself, and be ready to comfort His heart, His grieving heart—then only, with tearful eyes, will God trust you and love you. If you are ready to die, if you cry out to God, "Whatever place you have for us to die, I will go to that place, and I am ready to deny myself, I am ready to die in the place of other people for the sake of Your cause," and if you really dash to that point, ready to sacrifice yourself, then God may be able to trust you. In that case, you are in a position similar to that of Jesus, praying in the garden of Gethsemane: "My Father, if it is possible, let this cup pass from me; nevertheless, not as I will, but as thou wilt." And if you are utterly going to do things for the sake of God's will, then alone will He believe you. Even though He has been betrayed by so many people, when Jesus prayed before God, saying: "You may do anything You please, and I will follow You," then God could cry out to Jesus: "You resemble me; you restored yourself in the image and likeness of Myself." In that case alone, God can trust the person.

Even though God may have to lose the whole world, the whole nation, whole tribe, whole clan, whole family—if He has one person left with that kind of attitude, that devotion to the love of God, and oneness with God, forming the foundation in God's love, God will be pleased with that person. Starting right from that person, He can broaden the scope of His love and loving sphere, reaching out to the whole world again.

In other words, we must resemble God to the fullest extent. If we analyze God or dissolve God there will be one thing left, and that is love, God's love. We must be ready to sacrifice ourselves for this great love. Even if we may have to die on the sea, die on the mountainside, die in the deep valley of darkness, wherever we may have to die; or if we are killed by other persons for this great cause, we must be ready to do that, and this is going to be our determination. That is why in the Bible Jesus said, "Whoever wants to gain his life will lose it, and whoever is ready to lose his life for my sake, will gain it."

I hope that you consider these ideas seriously, and pray to God. He will answer you.

7

The Path
I Am Walking

July 20, 1984

On the Occasion of Departing for Danbury

My faith will not change, wherever I go! To say that your faith will never change means that your mind will never change. By the same token, the world that I am pursuing will not change, either. Wherever I go, whether it is a high place or a low one, my life will be the same life.

Since we do not have much time today, I would like to give you a very short and simple lecture. The work of God is to make unity. If there had been no fall, each man and woman would have experienced the unity of mind and body. Then with the unity of man and woman in marriage, the ideal would have been achieved.

However, the world in which we live has not yet become

one. The huge world is nothing more than the extension of individual men and women. Almost no one can claim that their mind and body are always united, thus the world in which we are living is not the world which God wanted. This is the fallen world, instead.

Since there are no individual men and women united perfectly in mind and body, there are no families which are perfect, and no societies, nations or world which are perfect. Whenever a person becomes perfectly united in mind and body, God relates with that person as one completed individual. When such men and women are united, then God becomes the subject or center of that couple. If a certain tribe becomes totally united, then God becomes the center or the subject of that particular tribe. Therefore, it makes no difference how large the population becomes because God wants to be the center and subject to everybody.

When God becomes the subject and center of every individual, the unified world comes into being. Within the unified world we would have the unified nation, unified communities, unified tribes, families and so forth. Do you think God would like to travel around the world for sight-seeing once the unification of the world has been achieved? Or would He be content to do that at some intermediate stage, perhaps the level of unified tribes or nations? What do you think? Certainly, God would want to wait to travel through the world until it is completely unified. I am sure God is thinking now that Reverend Moon understands His desire quite well!

What is the path I am walking? My ultimate mission as a son of God is to bring about the unity of the entire world. If there had been no fall, God would never have had any problem in visiting this world. All people would have become perfected and would have automatically welcomed God into this world. It would not have mattered how many billions of people were born; they would all have been incorporated into the unified world.

God has worked so hard to bring unity on the levels of

family, clan, tribe, nation and world. But if Adam and Eve had not fallen, they would have automatically created that unified family, clan, tribe, nation and world. If that was the reality, then God would be free to travel everywhere, joyfully experiencing unity. Wherever He would go, He would be with His people.

Because of the fall, barriers and division came into the world on every level. Now God has to deal with this divided world and that is the tragedy of both God and humanity. God is not at the center of this compartmentalized, divided world; instead, Satan is at the center and is running it. Incredible conflict pervades every relationship, first of all between the individual mind and body. Throughout history, no one has been able to pull out and eliminate the roots of conflict of this world.

There is conflict between men and women, between families, tribes, and nations. There is conflict between East and West. As the champion of division, Satan knows precisely how to divide this world. Therefore, a godly man must appear who has the power to bring unity and overcome the power of divisiveness. How much joy that would bring to God!

There have been many saints throughout history and they were always unifiers. In the face of adversity, they never allowed themselves to become divided. Among such people, the greatest of all was Jesus Christ. Jesus was the Son of God and he came to unite the world with the greatest power of unity that anyone has ever seen. He brought unity among all different races and cultures. Even his enemies, the forces of Satan who tried to destroy him, could be brought into unity by him. I want you to understand that Jesus prayed on the cross for his enemies because his deepest purpose and mission was to bring unity to everyone.

However, when Jesus was bearing the cross he was a single, solitary person. His disciples were not supporting Jesus; the chosen nation was not supporting him and the Roman Empire was not supporting him. He was absolutely alone. But today, what is Reverend Moon doing? Reverend

Moon came to this modern age to bring unity. He is a unifier—he is casting fire to bring about unity. Thus, no matter what we face, we will succeed. The forces of Satan are trying to divide the Moonies and they are trying to divide Christianity, but they cannot do it.

The entire world is watching the Unification Church and Reverend and Mrs. Moon. Many people are curious about Mrs. Moon and how she is taking the recent turn of events. Also they are wondering if the Unification Church is now shattered into pieces and destroyed. But on the contrary, under these difficult circumstances the Unification Church has found itself most powerful. If my wife sheds tears, they are not the tears of tragedy or defeat; they are the tears of unity, tears for bringing hope to the future.

God's method has always been that of being hit and then restoring it, over and over again throughout history. Thus we can sometimes weep knowing that our tears will bring us greater determination and hope to allow us to march forward to the greatest victory. But if we become defeatists we will never become the people who can receive the ultimate blessings from God. Those ultimate blessings can come only to those who endure being hit and never falter, those who continue to move forward.

Even though Reverend Moon is opposed by the entire United States, I will never be defeated. I am ready to receive the blessing that goes far beyond any blessing of this country. We are growing every day—today we are greater than yesterday and tomorrow will be greater than today. If God provides a way for me to bring about the unity of the 4.5 billion people of this world, I will not hesitate an instant to take that path.

When the Supreme Court rejected our review on May 14, I never wavered in asking God, "What way do You want to lead us now?" Since then, in the past two months great numbers of Christians have become united. Today I am going the road of incarceration and I am asking God, "What is Your next chapter for me? Let Your will be done and bring the unity of all humankind, centering upon the True

Parents." I know that no matter where I go, I will find people who will follow; strangers will follow me, even beyond the Unification Church.

When I walk over the hill, the unified world will be waiting there to welcome me. The billions of people will become united into one. There is a way for God to come and dwell with humankind. For the first time, the unity between God and ourselves will be achieved.

Therefore I walk the road of the cross with hope and a totally victorious mind. We are here together, people from all different cultures and the five different colors of skin. You must be united as you follow me. You parents with children must follow me with your entire family united. All the members throughout the world must follow in unity; that is the only way you can follow me. Because of this momentous day, there is great hope for unity starting from the membership of the Unification Church and spreading out to the rest of humanity. Because of this day, unity shall become a reality. It will continue to grow, greater and greater.

This is a glorious, victorious and historical day. For that reason, I don't want you to send me off in tears. If you have tears automatically streaming down your face, they must not be tears of tragedy. They must be tears of determination, telling me, "Trust us. We are going to bring 100 times greater victory in the days to come." I want you to understand that if you have sadness in your heart today, there is only one way to alleviate it. On the day that I return, you must be able to share with me about all the thousands of people who became united while I was gone. That is the only way you can be worthy of your tears.

I am going the road of confinement for the purpose of unity. Inside the prison I will work even harder to bring about greater unity within the Unification movement and the Christian community. Also I am working to bring unity between the Unification movement, the Christian community, and other religions. That is the purpose of my going to prison today.

Therefore, I want all of you to unite. Unless you have that internal unity, you are inviting hell to come in. When you are united, every door in the world will be opened to you.

When Jesus was crucified, he went into hell first and opened the doors there. Today I am bearing my cross, but I will not die; I will open the doors of hell as a living person. From that point on, resurrection and Pentecost will come. That is the way I understand the meaning of this day.

The living God never dies. Therefore, my cross will only bring unification and victory. The doors to 120 nations shall be opened from today forward, depending upon how much you act. Today I am going as a champion, to bring the unity of all of humanity, as well as the unity of heaven and earth.

You must inherit my spirit and tradition. That means you must also become unifiers, becoming united among yourselves and helping others to unite. Even our mass weddings, such as that of the six thousand couples, are symbolic examples of my work to bring unity between people from all the six continents, with different language, culture and skin colors. The Unification Church members are one in heart. Our goal is to fulfill the will of God and the will of God is to bring the unity of all people. We are marching toward that goal!

The road of suffering and the cross shall have no power over me. I confront all difficulties and shatter them with my determination. I am opening the highway to the horizon of hope and beyond, all the way to the victory. Even if the time comes to give up my life, it will be given up for the unity of humankind. Then God will erect a monument to me as the champion of unity. Certainly anyone who died under such circumstances would be launched like a rocket directly into God's heart. Therefore, do not worry.

When Jesus was carrying the cross, he told people not to weep for him. Instead, he told them to weep for their children, their own people and nation and the world. Jesus could see the misery that would come to the world. I want you to understand that although there are only a few people here listening to me today, there are great numbers of people around the world who are shedding their tears in prayer, pouring out their hearts for the sake of God's will.

Have I been waging a futile battle? No, as I struggled for this seemingly impossible dream, I knew that the entire world would eventually rally around me. From now on, you can go out and shout to the world and everyone's heart shall be melted. Their consciences will be awakened and you will be able to unite them with your heart.

As we work for greater levels of unification, we will have greater levels of success; we will not decline. At this time, I am going away and you must stay here. This is your moment of commitment to become the catalyst for the unity of the world. The Unification Church is not alone; there are many other people and groups who are siding with us now. The time has come that people will stop mocking and scorning you for being a Moonie. Now you will be admired and you will be recognized as having a great spiritual leader. This is our own time of unification. We must stand up now and move forward to achieve our goals.

When the morning comes, the beautiful sunrise can be seen in the eastern sky. I want you to understand that the sunrise is now coming to the world. Now the sunbeams are becoming stronger and stronger and we will march forward forevermore. First we must ignite the sunshine of the individual; then the individual ignites the sunshine of the family and then the sunshine of the nation, and ultimately of the world and the universe. This is how we will grow.

Thus there is no time to rest and certainly no time to weep and be despairing. We have only one road to go—the road of determination and marching forward. Why is that? It is because we are the champions who must liberate God through unification. From that point of liberation, we will be able to take true dominion over the creation. From that point forward, the Kingdom of God on earth shall become a reality. I know that to my bones. That is the goal toward which I am marching today.

So far, we have prepared a container; now we are preparing something to put into that container—the victory of God. I am at the forefront of the marching lines, carrying that container. I merely am marching in the front of that line, but everybody behind me is going in the same direction with the same purpose. You and I have the same mission of world unity—that is the job we must do. I am going to open the doors of hell so while I am doing that, you must take care of this world. Unification is your sublime duty and your goal.

I want you to understand that I am going to prison on the worldwide level at this time. I have already gone to prison on the individual level, the family and the national level. This is my destiny. Jesus told his people, if you want to follow me, follow me with your cross. Therefore, if you want to follow Reverend Moon, you must bear the worldwide cross. Once you are victorious with the worldwide cross, you can come to visit me. After you have been victorious in carrying your own cross, then I will be able to come out of prison. I want you to understand that.

When I was in the North Korean prison, my mother came to visit me. She had walked many hundreds of miles, all the way across the peninsula, and the moment she saw me, she began to cry very strongly. At that point, I shouted out to my own mother, calling her by her given name, not mother, "I am not just your son. I have only come to this world through you. I am a son of God—you gave birth to me, so you should be as great as your son. You cannot be cowardly or weak. You must walk forward courageously and encourage me."

Today I am saying the same thing to you. Do not ever behave in a weak or cowardly fashion. You must be proud and courageous. Even without your encouragement, I will follow the highest possible road of a son of God. Thus, instead of trying to come and visit me, go out to the battlefield. Go out and bring unity to the world. Do not waste your time visiting me at the prison but bring the victory for God in the world.

Now show me your determination by standing and giving three cheers!